Books Under her Pen Name, Enyla

Enyla, *Survival Guide Through Self-Esteem*, Using Inherent Strengths to Promote Self-Worth, Self-Esteem Editor, Montréal, 2020.

Enyla, *Remember who you are!* Tome 1, The School of Life Serie, Montréal, Self-Esteem Editor, An ebook, 2015.

French Books with Editing Houses and Self-publishing

Aline Lévesque, *Guide de survie par l'estime de soi : pleins pouvoirs sur ma valeur*, illustrations de Julie Payette, Brossard, Éditions Un monde différent, 2020, 288 pages.

Aline Lévesque, *La mort et moi : anecdotes savoureuses sur ma vie au salon funéraire et après*, Brossard, les Éditions Estime-Plus, 2019, 128 pages.

Aline Lévesque, *Rappelle-toi qui tu es !* Brossard, les Éditions Estime-Plus, 2014, 82 pages.

Aline Lévesque, *Pour l'amour de vos enfants, ne dormez pas avec eux.* Boucherville, Béliveau Éditeur, 2012, 304 pages.

Aline Lévesque, *Mission ? Passions ! par le fil d'Ariane*, Brossard, Éditions Un monde différent, 2007, 192 pages.

Aline Lévesque et Hedwidge Flückiger, *La Tendresse : chemin de guérison des émotions et du corps par la psycho-kinésiologie, science de la tendresse*, Brossard, Éditions Un monde différent, 2004, 208 pages.

Aline Lévesque, *Guide de survie par l'estime de soi : apprendre à être bon pour soi*, préface de Germain Duclos, illustrations de Julie Payette, Brossard, Éditions Un monde différent, 2000, 244 pages.

Aline Lévesque, *Si j'avais su…*, Saint-Hubert, Éditions Un monde différent, 1991, 142 pages.

SURVIVAL
GUIDE
THROUGH
SELF-ESTEEM

www.alinelevesque.com

Cover, Book design and layout:
Christian Campana / campana@christiancampana.com

Design of illustrations: Julie Payette

First translation: Donald O'hara

Translation of the 2020 edition
Rewriting and revision along with American English:
Clara Daigneault

Published by Self-Esteem Editor
Montréal, Canada

Legal deposit last quarter 2020
Bibliothèque et Archives nationales du Québec
Library and Archives Canada

ISBN/Soft cover 978-2-9814973-9-0
ISBN/EPUB   978-2-9819507-0-3

Printed in Canada and Printed on demand

ENYLA

SURVIVAL GUIDE THROUGH SELF-ESTEEM

Using Inherent Strengths to Promote Self-Worth

Easy-to-apply
innovative techniques
by a self-esteem specialist

SELF-ESTEEM EDITOR

To Stephan,
the spouse of my days,
the friend of my life,
the proof that I deserve to be loved.

Table of contents

~

TABLES

Foreword

Why am I interested in self-esteem? The answer is both personal and professional.

Self-Esteem: My Life Preserver

My interest in self-esteem developed above and beyond my professional expertise; in fact, it happened out of necessity... For the first 35 years of my life, my personal development was entirely centered on my lack of self-esteem. As a joke, I often say that this journey should have earned me at least one or two honorary doctorates.

I did a lot of soul-searching, striving to prove that I was worthy, so much so that I became a workaholic. Starved for success, I wanted to uncover the secret of successful people and for years, I read them, studied them and mingled with them. It took a long time to sink in, but I finally learned that I was the only one responsible for the results that I had achieved. I realized that my false beliefs had created my rollercoaster of a life.

During a particularly overwhelming time in my life, I had lost my bearings and found myself near rock bottom. I was on the verge of drowning due to burnout, and I was looking for something to hold on to, which is where my analogy of the life preserver comes from. I finally accepted that my false beliefs in regard to my self-worth and my right to succeed had to change: having stronger self-esteem is how I would ensure my survival.

There's an adage that says, "We teach best what we most need to learn"... Indeed, self-esteem is like Ariane's thread, guiding me on my mission.

Moved by a Mission to Teach

Initially creating workshops for women, I have offered different personal development programs for decades. As a life coach, I have integrated various techniques that have allowed me to forge links between organizational psychology and psychokinesiology, neuro-linguistic programming (NLP), creative visualization, symbolism and naturopathy.

I had the privilege of speaking at the International Council of Self-Esteem in San Francisco, where I rubbed shoulders with pioneers in self-esteem development, including Nathaniel Branden, Chris Mruk and Robert Reasoner. I founded Césame, a program for improving the self-esteem of parents and children, aged 2 to 5, given throughout the province of Québec. I am also pleased to collaborate with "Mouvement santé mentale Québec" (A mental health organization in Québec, Canada).

Having built up a strong knowledge base, I wanted to share my experience outside of my workshops. This desire led to the creation of a group of self-esteem development counselors in Quebec. It also pushed me to begin writing, hoping to reach even more people who needed support in improving their self-esteem. That is how this survival guide came into being.

In this guide, I will share some of the most significant parts of my personal life, with utmost sincerity. *They will appear in italics.*

Using Inherent Strengths to Promote Self-Worth and Happiness

I could have used the word "strength" in the singular form, but by extending it to the plural, I wanted to emphasize that everyone naturally possesses multiple strengths, multiple capabilities.

Each person knows that they have inherent strengths; however, in the same way that a car can have a powerful engine, it can also be left parked, unused. People know that they possess these strengths, but like a ship with furled sails in a strong wind, they are unable to move forward.

This new edition allows me to highlight the latest advances, revealing how YOUR inherent strengths can influence:

- Your personal happiness;
- Awareness of your self-worth;
- The five "senses" of self-esteem;
- Every sphere of your life;
- Your brain's connections;
- Your genetic background (DNA) by way of your behavior;
- Your mental, and by extension, physical health.

You will also learn about:

- The confirmed, direct relationship between self-esteem and mental health.

- Epigenetics and brain plasticity and their role in effective mental programming.

- The complete lexicon of positive programming linked to ensuring and maintaining self-esteem.

Are you in need of a lifeline to free you from anxiety? Addiction? Anger? Misfortune? Defeatism? Dark thoughts? If so, this book is for you!

This guide is for anyone searching for inner wellbeing AND motivated to reach out and take hold of their destiny.

To do so, you will need to use your INHERENT STRENGTHS!

Wishing you smooth sailing on your life's odyssey!

Enyla

User Guide

This book, first and foremost, is intended to be an exchange with the reader *on what self-esteem is* and *how to develop it* in daily life to overcome obstacles, but also to welcome and take advantage of the beautiful, precious moments that we so easily forget to appreciate in the fast-paced lives we lead.

TYPES OF INFORMATION

As a guide, it includes different types of information:

- **Theory** in the **first** and **second** chapters;
- Self-assessment **exercises** in self-esteem in the chapter 3;
- **Techniques and tools** to help develop your self-esteem in the chapters 4 and 5.
- **Real stories** experienced by me or by my workshop attendees.

READING METHODS

Depending on what kind of a reader you are, here are a few of the potential reading methods:

1. Of course, you may read the **entire** book from cover to cover and **do the exercises** as they appear.
2. You may also decide to go for the theory portion without doing the exercises.
3. My clients' experiences can be read first or reread on occasion. Their names are written in **bold** (**Carole** or **Peter**), to indicate where their **personal stories** begin. Of course, their names have been changed to protect their privacy. As for my experiences, they will be written in italics and centered between flourishes.

4. You may also decide to **only** do the **exercises** (chapter 3).

5. Be sure to start a paper or digital workbook for all your notes, particularly for the exercises, as this will serve as your own **expedition journal**.

6. The suggested **techniques** will be indicated by a **check mark:** ✔ and the **tools** by a life preserver: 🛟

Above all, it is important to remember to use this book as a reference to help you through the various stages of your life. Let it be your guidebook, lighthouse, or lifeline if necessary.

Introduction

Feeling Unique

The main objective of this book is to make you feel UNIQUE, SPECIAL! Let is also offering you a passport for your physical and mental well-being.

To that end, my intention is to provide you with the essential information, the practical tools for those who are currently experiencing problems and who are trying to find themselves or find meaning in their life and who want to survive. This guide is also for anyone who wishes to develop their potential and their autonomy.

Inspired by wilderness survival guides, I have drawn a parallel, psychologically speaking, between what happens on a wildlife excursion and what happens in the life you lead. This is why, throughout this book, I compare life to a long expedition, where your basic equipment is your self-esteem. In order to succeed on the journey of life, I invite you to go through the stages of preparation and survival in the same way that an excursionist would.

"Survival" can be defined in three different ways in the dictionary. The first means to stay alive, to live longer in relation to an event, such as an illness or accident. The second pertains to life after death. For our purposes, we will use the third definition from the military, which establishes the possibility of survival in hostile and dangerous situations. "*It is the equipment which ensures survival, the required physical training, as well as the instructions given to those most likely to face such situations.*"

To have the will to survive, it is necessary to understand the meaning of life. To reach the point of having the willpower to "survive at all costs", we must rediscover that inner, vital energy which may sometimes lie dormant, but is irrevocably present in each one of us.

This guide will open up new avenues for you or remind you of previously acquired *survival techniques* in this particular time of your life when you need to hear them anew.

These techniques will cover different stages, in order to:

- Better understand the meaning of life and adequately prepare yourself for this long journey to reach your destination port;

- Become aware of who you *really* are and celebrate yourself;

- Take charge of yourself to face the "seasons of life";

- Guide you on your own path and provide you with practical tools for self-motivation.

The Starting Point of This Long Journey: You!

You are extraordinary and unique. Nobody has the same fingerprints as you, nor the same genetic code, the same role, or the same mission in life. YOU ARE THE ONLY ONE WHO IS EXACTLY LIKE YOU!

Albert Jacquard once said: "Each human being is unique and unclassifiable. There is giftedness in every human being." Every time I heard similar statements in the past, this little voice inside my head would say: "That might apply to others, but I don't really see what is so special about me... It would be misplaced pride on my part to believe that!"

Perhaps you tell yourself similar things, such as "Come on! I'm just ordinary, pretty well like everyone else." Or: "I really don't see how I'm unique in any way."

Still others are ready to believe it, as if speaking of a far-off treasure waiting to be discovered, but with absolutely no idea which road to take to find it.

Regardless of the rational objections you may come up with in relation to the statement, "*You are an extraordinary and unique person,* " I nevertheless encourage you to adopt this attitude like yours IMMEDIATELY. Do so even if you have to pretend to believe it for the time being, while you are reading through this guide, right up until you have developed the belief that you truly are UNIQUE!

We cannot discover a treasure in which we do not believe. With the help of this guide, and through every stage of your life, I invite you to reach this destination of self-discovery, this *extraordinary you!*

THE GOAL

Make YOU feel UNIQUE
and to offer you a
PASSPORT FOR YOUR HEALTH!

CHAPTER 1

LIFE:
A LONG EXPEDITION

~

Dying or surviving depends on two factors:
the will to survive at all costs
and an in-depth knowledge
of survival techniques.[1]

~

1 Descheneaux, Jean-Georges (1990). *Guide pratique de survie en forêt canadienne.*
   (A Practical Survival Guide in Canadian Forests), p.16.

Life: An Expedition

Would you prepare yourself in the same way for a few hours trek as you would to climb Mount Everest? Your answer would probably be "Absolutely not!"

After having read the two factors related to survival in the wild, outlined on the previous page, I realized that they could easily be applied to life in general, since we must survive in every sense of the word. "Is survival not the same as everyday life with all the will to strive, energy and lucidity we all need?"

For that matter, taking into consideration the accelerated evolution of today's society, does each of us have the necessary equipment to survive this type of expedition, let alone a saga that will last a lifetime?

Despite the fact that the world's social condition continues to deteriorate, North America and Europe nonetheless are lucky enough to enjoy an acceptable quality of life where a large number of people are able to live and survive and have their basic needs met. Our social and political context allows us to live in peace, for one thing, without having to defend our territory with weapons every day, which is, as I am sure you will agree, a significant advantage.

It is thus within the context of an industrialized country that we will be working together to understand and travel through the course of modern-day life. However, regardless of where you live, survival obliges everyone to adopt the pertinent attitudes and the right tools to succeed. I hope the reflections or the advice that you find here will prove useful, even in very different environments.

Unprepared Life Excursionists

The following figures speak for themselves: A report from Quebec, Canada's provincial health organization[2], concluded that over 24% of the population (33% of women, 24% of men) experience high levels of psychological distress.

---

2   According to the Quebec Population Health Survey (Statistics Institute of Quebec, 2016).

This is higher than the percentage of people living with all physical illnesses combined. If we attempt to dissect this issue and identify its core components, we find social alienation, profound loneliness, and poor sense of self-esteem.

Thus, more than one person out of every four experiences inner suffering and lives a painful existence, often to the point of being non-functional: This means burnout, depression, or other serious illnesses. Yet, every day, you and I probably come across these people who are living with their own personal dramas and have no idea how serious this situation is. You yourself might even be one of them.

For the last 30 years, the province of Quebec has multiplied its efforts in prevention and public awareness. While it used to have the highest percent of teenage suicides in the country, since 2000, Quebec's suicide rate has significantly decreased. Today, it is in keeping with the national average.

Psychological distress spares no one and can affect people from all age groups: the elderly, the middle-aged, and teenagers; even children can be affected. The only way to escape life pressures is to find ways to manage them and maintain some sort of balance.

The Rules of the Game Have Changed

The philosophy of child rearing in which parental authority took precedence over anything else has been replaced with that of the spoiled child who has no rules or limitations. The sacred sense of family has slowly crumbled over time, contributing to the overall breakdown of families lost in a variety of models, which are still in need of exploration or definition. The cult of religion has also taken a powerful hit, and the prevailing anticlericalism has failed to fill this deep inner void. Uncertain economic conditions have destabilized the working world. Additionally, the fruitless search for panaceas, for universal remedies, has left people feeling disenchanted.

In short, our society has been hit with the devastating winds of change, which have left nothing, or so little in their wake that it is normal for people to feel disillusioned. A lot of people have had

> *Life is discovering, deep down, what we do not know about ourselves!*
> **Gilles Dault**

enough of their insipid existence and are looking to either find ways to compensate for the emptiness or put an end to it all.

But, Nature is vast, majestic, and born of nothing. It has proven many times over that it knows how to regenerate anew from devastated fields, burnt forests and ice storms.

And like Nature, of which we are all an integral part, we are living in this unique era when everyone must learn to rebuild themselves again, since the majority of the models we refer to no longer exist.

From these new values, these reformulated beliefs, we must once again find our way, our own path, and develop our self-esteem in order to regain our human dignity. The compass can be found within us. Therein lies the answer. Therein lies the true and abundant Source of Life. A revival for all.

The Ultimate Goal of the Journey

What is the ultimate goal of living a whole lifetime on this Earth? Why are we alive? Each individual undoubtedly has his or her own interpretation of life's final goal; this is a philosophical debate that has gone on for centuries. Of course, I do not pretend whatsoever to know THE answer to this age-old question. However, I would like to share with you the questions and answers on this topic that I have come across thus far in my life. They have allowed me to understand and consider that life is the most beautiful trip in the world, a wonderful odyssey, provided of course, that its ultimate meaning and goal are understood.

In my opinion, *succeeding in life* means remaining loyal to our deepest beliefs. The only true failure is when we betray our dreams and aspirations. Also, our life should be spent "discovering, deep down, what we don't know about ourselves," *the real me.*

Between Life and Death

When I was a teenager, my father changed careers and became the director of a funeral parlor. His decision was motivated by his great respect for death itself, and by his compassion for the bereaved. I had the opportunity, therefore, to live in a funeral home, as it made up half of our family's house. Believe me, being around death on a daily basis really gives meaning to life, though you still have to stop and think about it, of course.

We always had to lower our voices or the volume on the television or stop bickering with my brothers and sisters because there would be a deceased person and their family next door, separated from us by a thin wall. Hence my belief that death is part of life: there is only a wall between us!

Unfortunately, today's society hides the truth from children that we are all on a definite journey, with a beginning and an end, and this is true even if they are faced with this reality in their own entourage when they lose a grandparent, for example.

How can a parent or a guardian explain such a thing when they themselves know nothing about it? The concepts that we have learned, especially those that religion has taught us, are not necessarily satisfactory. Perhaps now is the time to think about finding the answers that make sense to you personally.

Our Lifeline

Let's suppose that point O represents the day you were born, and the square □ is the day you die. The line between these two points represents your entire life, let's say over an eighty-year lifespan.

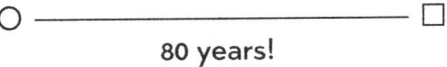

80 years!

Why is it that Madam A was more fulfilled compared to Mister B between the day of their birth and death? Between these two crucial moments, why did Mr. X succeed better in life than Ms. Y?

There no doubt exists a wide range of possible answers, all equally plausible. In my view, I would conclude that what makes the difference in achievement between one and the other comes from whether or not they took *responsibility* for their own lives.

You have surely known people who have no goals, or dreams or hopes, who are, in essence, lifeless inside. I think that these people are already dead in their own way, in their heart, mind and soul... They just will not be buried until years later, perhaps at 70 or 80 years old. It's so sad!

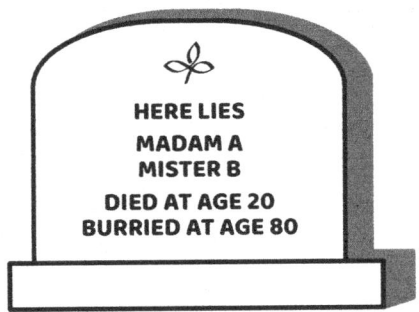

HERE LIES
MADAM A
MISTER B
DIED AT AGE 20
BURRIED AT AGE 80

Here, I encourage you to respond to this reflection in your paper or digital expedition journal.

Exercise: My Tombstone

Would you like the epitaph carved on your tombstone between your date of birth and death (for example, 1960–2040) to have true meaning? Even though tombstones are less common than they were, this exercise is still an important step in the process.

Take a few minutes to think it over, then put it in writing! What would you like people to say about you after your death or burial? What would you like to have accomplished? What would you like to have written about you on your tombstone? Take the time to do this exercise, which, while it may seem a bit macabre, usually has a very positive effect on those who do it because it relates to your personal mission in life. Try it and see!

The Results

If you have had the courage to do the exercise, you may have one of the following responses:

1. **Feeling Pleasantly surprised by your result:** You never expected that this / these element(s) that describe you would be so important to you. Your core values have been revealed, and they will be important to remember along your journey.

2. **Feeling skeptical about your result:** Were you surprised by what you wrote? If so, ask yourself, "Do you really care about what you just wrote?" Or is it more your current situation that leads you to want to be recognized in that way? Already by questioning your results, you are on the right track to discovering if your priorities are truly yours. Continue checking in with yourself to find the right road map.

3. **Feeling dissatisfied with your result.** If you did not find a satisfactory answer, do not panic! You probably have long enough to live for you to make significant changes and come back to this exercise later. Your life belongs to you; you are the captain of the ship.

Unable to Answer?

If you were unable to answer such a question, don't worry! It is possible that talking about death, your own in particular, brings about uncomfortable feelings that prevent you from thinking calmly about it. Give yourself time and come back to it later.

Perhaps your tendency is to perceive this exercise in terms of the opinion or image that people will have about you after your death.

> *The only real failure is to betray our aspirations and dreams, and to be unfaithful to that which we most deeply believe of ourselves!*

For that matter, it may not even bother you because what really counts is what you will think of yourself as you approach death, not what others think. If so, then you are quite right.

The main goal of this exercise is to demonstrate what YOU would like to hear by way of confirming your personal accomplishments at the end of your life and not based on someone else's evaluation.

If it makes it easier, do the exercise while asking yourself: *What words would explain why I lived this life?*

A Small Reflection on Life

Here are a few questions you can answer if you want to take stock in *the meaning of life*.

Questions	Very often	Occasionally	Never
Have you ever asked yourself these questions: "Why am I alive?" or, "What is life?"			
Do you have goals? If yes, are they specific? Are they written down? If not, why?			
Are you in very good physical health? Are you in good mental health?			
Do you know what your life's mission is?			
Are you happy?			
Do you know your life mission?			
Are you satisfied with your life so far?			
Do you have any religious or spiritual beliefs?			
Are you the *rebellious* type in reaction to life's events, or more *docile*?			
Is death a taboo subject that is best not to think about?			

There are no right or wrong answers. This exercise is *to help make you be aware of your position on the meaning of life* in general. Take the time to write your answers in your expedition journal; you can come back to them from time to time and follow the evolution in your way of thinking.

To conclude, how is life meaningful to you?

The Philosophy of Survival

In Preparation

We have already established that you would prepare yourself differently for a short hike versus climbing Mount Everest. Regardless of the destination or the kind of expedition you are undertaking, there are four essential factors you need in preparation, including

A. Understanding the type of excursion that is involved and learning the **basic principles** of survival;

B. Meticulously planning the **equipment** needed, as well as the physical and mental requirements;

C. Knowing **which direction to take** for the duration of the journey, as well as how to readjust in order to reach your destination;

D. A digital or paper **expedition journal** for you to take note of your evolution.

Legitimate Questions

After having faced some stormy times in their lives, here are some of the questions that my clients asked during individual interviews or during my workshops: Where can I find comfort? Where do I go? Who am I? What can I hold on to these turbulent times? Which compass should I rely on? Is there still a true North that I can believe in?

One Answer: Self-Esteem as a Life Preserver

The first crucial response to all of these questions as to which direction to take is *within ourselves!* Therein lies a rich and precious reserve, *a compass* that can be called our self-esteem; this source of indication is there to guide you towards a balanced life that is uniquely yours.

Knowing that the answer is inside us does not mean that consulting a specialist to help you find it is out of the question. But too often, too many people are looking for an easy or ready-made answer, a miracle cure for this age of "immediacy" that we live in.

They want an easy, external solution: a medication, body care products or services, a therapist that will "heal" them, a medium, vacations, etc.

Professionally, I act as a "coach" to help people develop their potential and start playing the best game of their life. For these efforts to produce the desired results, they must believe that they have the potential to begin with. In my practice, I have met a good many people who did not permit themselves the right to succeed, or even the right to exist. To give life meaning, you must first grant yourself the right to live this life in which you have the directing, producing and starring role all at the same time.

To access your treasure within, you need an essential key: the development of your self-esteem, which becomes a vital tool in the quest for the meaning of life and survival. Self-esteem is THE key to starting your voyage towards the real you, this unknown treasure. It is a LIFE preserver.

Developing your self-esteem, however, is not the solution to all of your personal problems. It is not "magical thinking", but it remains an essential basis for the ability to act, to take charge of your life and be successful. Without this deep conviction *that something wonderful awaits you* somewhere, even if it is a small aspiration that you deserve better, it's hard to progress, to move forward. No voyage is possible if we are convinced that we won't get anywhere.

A healthy self-esteem allows you to feel loved, unconditionally, and it will help you discover your real mission in life, "the dream of your soul."

Follow me on this life's journey filled with adventures, some of which may be exhausting for sure, but which will undoubtedly be thrilling. Understanding the destination, mastering the solutions to overcoming obstacles that are sure to arise, and knowing how to learn from them, that is life!

> *Understanding the destination, mastering the solutions to overcoming obstacles which are sure to arise, and knowing how to learn from them, that is life!*

CHAPTER 2

SELF-ESTEEM: AS A COMPASS

∽

SELF-ESTEEM
is the awareness
of our personal worth
that we acknowledge
in different areas of our life.[3]

∽

---

3   Definition adopted by the Quebec Association of Intervention Workers for the Development of Self-Esteem.

Self-Esteem: As a Compass

In keeping with our analogy of survival in the wilderness—and as we said previously—we can consider self-esteem as a compass which will point to magnetic north, just as the needle of a compass would. For our purpose, we'll define magnetic north as our *true self* and our self-esteem then becomes our basic equipment to give us directions or to indicate when we have strayed off course.

Self-Esteem in Theory

Over the past few years, more and more, studies and research on self-esteem have been conducted and their definitions are becoming more refined. Some specialists have used the term self-concept or self-image; each adding to or further specifying their characteristics, according to their point of view or research interests.

Here is a simple and concrete definition: "Self-esteem is the awareness of our personal worth that we acknowledge in different areas of our life[4]." Therefore, this corresponds to a set of attitudes, self-perceptions and beliefs that cause us to act and react to the various circumstances in our lives. In other words, it's the reputation that we have of ourselves.

I would like to specify that using the word "awareness" in relation to value does not refer to the *true value* of the person, but rather to their *self-concept*; this situation is subjective and often leads to very different perceptions of reality. **Positive self-esteem** implies self-worth that is a **realistic** assessment of our capabilities and limitations, while low self-esteem implies a diminished or amplified sense of self-worth.

---

4   Ibid.

Comparing Different Concepts

We will now compare a few of the most common concepts, as well as ones that can sometimes be confusing.

SELF-IMAGE

SELF-IMAGE refers to a series of beliefs and mental images that we hold about who we are as a person. This general perception includes our physical appearance as well. It constitutes a kind of personal assessment that can be summed up globally as: "Overall, I'm OK", "I'm good", "I'm ugly", "I'm great".

The concept of SELF-IMAGE is really interesting and the first books that I read on the subject literally blew me away at the time. Dr. Maxwell Maltz, a renowned cosmetic surgeon, compiled extensive data on his patients' self-image *before* and *after* their life-changing, beauty-enhancing surgery. He concluded that a great many of his patients continued to see themselves as they had BEFORE the operation despite their new nose, ears, etc., as repugnant, and often devalued themselves. His clients could not integrate their new reality even with their enhancements; their self-perception remained negative.

There is thus an undeniable link between our self-image, and the value we attribute ourselves.

SELF-CONFIDENCE

As for SELF-CONFIDENCE, it is an attitude that demonstrates our assurance and ability to positively face obstacles and challenges. This means it relates more to our skills and abilities in performing certain activities.

For example, if in your workplace you are asked to help organize an activity you have already done, or if you have organized something similar in the past, you will feel confident and probably agree to the task feeling convinced that you will succeed.

When we talk about CONFIDENCE, we often hear something similar to: "I am able to…" or: "I might as well try before saying I can't succeed!" Note the optimism or hope for a favorable outcome. It is also important to emphasize that people who demonstrate the most self-confidence will usually have an easier time trusting others.

Self-confidence and self-esteem are interdependent, but should not be confused with one another. Self-confidence is an integral part of self-esteem. I will come back to this in more detail after I have finished defining more of these concepts.

SELF-LOVE

To describe the concept of SELF-LOVE, I often draw a parallel with people in love. Perhaps you are currently in love? Or you probably remember a time when you were. Did you place any conditions on this love? Probably not, at least at the beginning; you loved unconditionally! This is the case with SELF-LOVE when we accept ourselves unconditionally; in my opinion, this is a process that may last our whole lifetime, or just about.

Some people talk a lot about *self-respect* or *dignity*; in fact, *self-love* is the emotional dimension of self-esteem.

There is a distinction between *love* and *esteem*. Essentially, you could hold someone's qualities in high esteem, without actually loving them. The same principle can be applied to yourself. However, you cannot love yourself without having esteem for yourself.

SELF-ESTEEM

SELF-ESTEEM, as we saw earlier, is defined by the value that we attribute to ourselves and our sense of dignity, that is, whether we feel worthy of being loved, of being successful, etc. These types of sentences: "I deserve to be loved", "I believe that someone can love me...", "I was born to succeed" reflect a healthy self-esteem.

In fact, the latest research studies tend to define self-esteem from two separate axes:

1. Self-esteem in relation to self (respect, dignity, personal values);

2. Self-esteem in relation to actions (confidence, capability, choices, learning).

"Self-esteem is entirely inner working, carried out through one's self-image, their inner dialogue and through their feelings[5]".

According to psychiatrists André and Lelord, "Self-esteem is based on three ingredients: self-confidence, self-vision, self-love. The right dose of each of these components is essential to obtaining a harmonious self-esteem.[6]"

---

5   A synthesis from: Monbourquette, Jean (1996). *Je suis aimable, je suis capable: parcours pour l'estime et l'affirmation de soi (I am loveable, I am capable: route for the self-esteem and self-affirmation)* and from Nathaniel Branden's address given at the International Self-Esteem Council in San Francisco, June 2000.

6   André, Christophe & Lelord, François (2007). *Self-Esteem, Liking Yourself in Order to Live Better With Others.*

Self-esteem has nothing to do with the euphoric feeling hat you may have about yourself, nor does it have to do with your possessions or any cosmetic surgery you may have, even if today's advertising would have you believe otherwise.

Finally, certain behaviors can serve as clues to others as to whether you have good self-esteem. Yet, beyond the social masks that you have created for yourself, you alone are really aware of how you love and respect yourself.

Pointed Questions

In your opinion, can we have self-confidence and low self-esteem at the same time?

Absolutely! Some people show great self-confidence, demonstrating their skills and showing unfailing courage at times. Their energy or accomplishments are the envy of the more faint-hearted, but that does not necessarily mean that they have high self-esteem.

Why is that? It happens that some people wear a mask of "overconfidence" to camouflage their lack of self-esteem; they try to increase their self-worth in their own eyes, as well as those of others, by overachieving. They are motivated to take action, if you will, but without loving or respecting themselves. The major downside is that these people are seriously damaging their physical and mental health, and in many cases, are heading straight for a burnout.

Conversely, can we have good self-esteem but low self-confidence?

No way! Self-confidence is definitely linked to our self-worth. It is the most visible component of self-esteem. Thus, anyone with a healthy self-esteem demonstrates a good dose of self-confidence.

What Does Not Count as Self-Esteem: Too Much or Too Little

Having too much or too little self-esteem means that we overestimate or underestimate our abilities and limitations. In such cases, you might be rushing headlong into life or feel paralyzed by the weight of existence. That is why bragging, smugness, selfishness and self-centeredness should never be confused with self-esteem.

Balanced self-esteem carries a *realistic* evaluation of who we really are. In this sense, you feel good about yourself, and able to take on life's challenges with confidence, as well as set attainable goals for yourself.

Advantages and Disadvantages

It can be said that healthy self-esteem is the basis of our overall health, both physically and mentally. In a way, it is the cornerstone that greatly influences our behavior in all spheres of our life.

Low self-esteem comes with some of the following disadvantages:

- Predisposes you to all kinds of problems: physical health, emotional health;

- Increases your stress level and overall vulnerability;

- Increases the risk of having difficult relationships or being socially maladjusted.

LOW SELF-ESTEEM MAY PREDISPOSE YOU TO SERIOUS PROBLEMS	
In children, we observe:	**In teenagers, we witness:**
✓ Dropping out of school.	✓ Delinquency.
✓ Difficulties in social relationships, which can even go as far as violence towards themselves or others.	✓ Drug or alcohol abuse.
	✓ Pregnancy.
	✓ Depression.

Signs of Weak Versus Healthy Self-Esteem

Through my workshops over the years, I have sketched a profile of people who have and do not have healthy self-esteem. Here is a list of behaviors that are indicative of low or healthy self-esteem.

Perhaps you want to check some of your behaviors that can serve as indicators of the quality of your self-esteem. You can spontaneously check off the ones that you can relate to once you've reproduced them in your expedition journal.

Signs of a Weak Self-Esteem	✓	Signs of a Healthy Self-Esteem	✓
Is easily offended		Self-control	
Sensitivity to rejection and criticism		Easily receives compliments and criticism alike	
Easily criticizes others, makes reproachful remarks		Easily gives compliments and rejoices in others' success	
Pities themselves (victimhood), always complaining		Sense of responsibility	
"It's not my fault" attitude, blames others		Ability to recognize their mistakes	
Feels they are not loved or loveable ("No one can love me")		Ability to maintain harmonious social relations and friendships	
Excessive need for attention and approval		Ability to prioritize and express their own needs	
Inability to receive (gifts, compliments, etc.)		Believes they deserve the finer things in life	
No close friends		Capacity to maintain friendly and socially harmonious relationships	
Tendency to be unable to take care of themselves		Ability to prioritize their own needs	
Excessive dedication		Accepts their limits	
Desires to win at all cost		Ability to adapt	
Propensity to place themselves in a situation of failure or sabotage their own success		Believes they deserve success	
Selfishness		Personal integrity	
Contempt (for themselves or for others)		Confidence in themselves and in others	
Pessimism or defeatist attitudes		Optimism and "joie de vivre"	
Indecisive or doubts themselves		Ability to make the right decisions	

Signs of a Weak Self-Esteem	✓	Signs of a Healthy Self-Esteem	✓
Aggressiveness		Assertiveness, without being aggressive	
Rigid thinking		Open-mindedness	
Procrastination		Usually acts quickly	
Boasting		Recognizes their strengths and limitations	
Signs of depression not linked to specific events (anxiety, drop in self-worth, etc.)		Good level of physical and mental energy	
Fears success or has great difficulty succeeding		Used to setting realistic goals	
Fear of failure or repeat failures		Ability to deal with stressful situations	
Substance Abuse (alcohol, drugs)		Moderation	
Escapism		Ability to face problems	
Depression		Takes charge of their mental well-being	
Suicide or suicide attempts		Propensity to live according to their values, to manage obstacles and be hopeful	

Well-balanced self-esteem will:

⬆ Increase your resistance to stress;

⬆ Increase your energy level to better manage and overcome obstacles;

⬆ Help you persevere in pursuing projects;

⬆ Ensure better interpersonal relationships.

Anyone with good self-esteem knows how to: command respect, feel in charge of their life, take ownership of it and be able to enjoy it even more.

No matter how you may have felt in the past about your self-esteem, it is something that can be developed at any age. Do not believe the old saying that "you can't teach an old dog new tricks". Germain Duclos, a specialist on the subject, affirms rather, "Anything is possible as long as you're alive." That is to say that nothing is lost; be optimistic!

At What Age Is Self-Esteem Formed?

Studies show that self-esteem, being a personal value judgment, can only develop around the age of seven or eight. According to cognitive psychology, this corresponds to the age of reason with the appearance of logical thinking and the ability to make rational judgments.

As for younger children from birth to eight years of age, we speak in terms of pre-esteem. We need to bear in mind, however, that during all of these years, we foster either *favorable or unfavorable attitudes* related to our children's self-esteem. This explains why this period is so important because it is also during this time that children's deep wounds related to rejection or to their dignity are imprinted.

The Roots of Self-Esteem

Self-esteem is rooted in the bond that occurs between an infant and his mother or other significant people; it is gradually built up over the years through these bonds of attachment and through various life-changing experiences from an early age.

All the months of conception, the birth itself, then the parent's gaze, the loving care, the cuddles, and adequate responses to the baby's crying are all essential building blocks for nurturing a child's psychological needs.

Studies show that it is from these very early bonds of attachment that children build the basis of their relationship with themselves (their self-esteem) and with others. Also, the emotional security developed in this emotional bond is the prerequisite for positive self-esteem.

A child must feel secure first, before being able to experience a detachment from the parent without any problem, even temporarily. Conversely, the emotional insecurity related to this stage of life and the ensuing difficulties will be the basis for insufficient self-esteem.

Cases

Stephany is a single mother who experienced incest. I got to know her at my self-esteem workshops for parents and children. She is someone who is very anxious, which leads to her being overprotective of her five-year-old daughter. In fact, Stephanie *does everything for her daughter*, she smothers her: she never leaves her side, lets her sleep in her bed and was even planning to move in front of the school now that her daughter is old enough to attend, so as to protect her from any eventuality.

It is obvious that the behavior of such an anxious parent can only be detrimental to the child's perception of herself. Her identity and abilities are totally tied to her mother. When she comes to detach herself from her, a huge void will be created and the child's self-esteem will end up being deficient.

As far as I'm concerned, during my therapy sessions, I was able to relive the feelings of rejection that I had experienced from my mother at various times in my early childhood, from birth until the age of four. Very strong feelings permeated my body and soul, forming the basis of the negative self-perception that stayed with me for many years.

By this testimony, I am not trying to blame my mother, or to overwhelm all the working moms or the ones that are discouraged at one point or another of their motherhood. Instead, my story should be read as my very personal life's journey, which has turned out to be "my path" to grow on this earth.

The Cycles of Self-Esteem

According to the Life Cycles

In itself, self-esteem is not a static, fixed element. On the contrary, everyone will see their self-esteem fluctuate in various ways over the course of their life. First, because of age itself, it is normal that our self-esteem is not the same at 18 as it is at 50. Each stage of life: childhood, adolescence, adulthood, retirement, brings its share of improvement, and sometimes deterioration, of our self-esteem. This can be explained by the fact that life experiences play positively or negatively on our self-perception, according to which path we are on. **Self-esteem needs to be regularly activated in order to keep its value;** throughout this book, you will find various methods to help you do so.

For example, a person who has experienced a number of successes in their life, and only a few failures, can certainly have higher self-esteem than someone who has suffered a series of consecutive failures. This is, however, no guarantee; it all depends on the individual's perception of their successes.

Table: "The Evolution of Self-esteem According to Life Cycles"

This table shows the different stages of self-esteem according to age and the elements that define them.

THE EVOLUTION OF SELF-ESTEEM ACCORDING TO LIFE CYCLES[7]

Age	Stage	Defined by
0–8	Pre-esteem	The perspective of significant people
8–12	Appearance of self-esteem	The perspective of oneself
12–20	Consolidation of self-esteem	The transition from the perspective of parents to the peers
Adult	Management of self-esteem	The perspective of oneself and from peers

Pre-esteem is what develops between birth and age 8 and stems from the recognition received via important people in the life of the child you once were. Between 8 and 12, the development of your own self-esteem happened through the assessment you began to make of yourself.

As a teenager, you consolidated what you learned through the recognition of your peers, who at this stage, carried a lot more weight than that of your parents.

As an adult, you are able to manage your self-esteem first from your own perspective, and then from other people's. You must understand, however, that no one can give you better esteem than yourself.

For many years, I had the tendency to think that I was stubborn. When I mentioned this to the vice-president of a company whom I had been working with for a few months, he made me realize that I had the wrong impression of myself. He had seen my determination, of course, but also my constant openness to new ideas that were offered to enhance my proposals. From then on, thanks to his realistic view of me, I was able to adjust my own perception of myself, which raised my self-esteem.

---

7   Inspired from: Fafard, Jacques (1997). L'estime de soi et l'intervention (Self-Esteem and Intervention), Défi-Jeunesse, vol IV, no 2.

According to the Different Aspects of Life

Self-esteem can fluctuate within the same individual according to the different aspects of their life, namely physical, social, artistic, school, family and professional. For example, you may have high self-esteem in relation to your professional skills, but your self-esteem may be much lower when it comes to your appearance.

Or you may recognize your skills as valid in sports activities, but if you are asked to sing, then you may feel as if you have lower self-esteem because you don't believe in your musical talents.

The Best Inheritance

One thing is for sure, a good, healthy genetic background is enviable and desirable for all of us. The same goes for self-esteem; it is one of the most precious gifts a parent can leave their child.

Studies have shown that self-esteem is the main factor in preventing adjustment problems and learning difficulties in children,[8] as well as mental illness in adults: this is to say that it is crucially important to gift our children, along with the children in our environment, as well as ourselves.

The adults in a child's life have the opportunity to intervene in the development of their self-esteem. Every child needs to live with parents or significant people in their life who are comfortable in their own skin: parents, teachers, coaches, etc. Unfortunately, reality does not always correspond with this ideal.

---

8   Duclos, Germain (2001). *Quand les tout-petits apprennent à s'estimer... pour favoriser l'estime de soi des enfants de 3 à 6 ans.* (When toddlers learn to value themselves... fostering self-esteem in children aged 3 to 6).

The Five Senses
of Self-Esteem

Origins of the Theory

The originator of the theory, Mr. Robert Reasoner[9], designed a self-esteem program for the American school system, which was also adapted for the Canadian context.

The approach is simple, and easy to understand and evaluate. This is why many educational and social institutions have adopted it in recent years. I, for one, appreciate the practicality of these Five Senses when it comes to working on our self-esteem in a concrete way.

According to Reasoner's program, self-esteem develops from the following five senses:

- A Sense of Security;

- A Sense of Identity;

- A Sense of Belonging;

- A Sense of School Achievement: the pursuit of goals;

- A Sense of Social Skills: a problem-solving process.

For children, the development of these senses progresses in a particular way. From birth, when the infant's natural, basic needs are met, they are living in a context that promotes their sense of security. Then, the parent's attention, regard, and availability will contribute to the child's sense of identity so that the child becomes aware of his strengths and limitations. Later on, particularly during the teenage years, the sense of belonging towards a family or group of friends develops. As for the sense of academic success and the sense of

---

9   Reasoner, Robert (1988). Building Self-Esteem Program.

social skills, these develop during the learning years at school and within the child's social circles.

Since my work has been primarily with adults, I preferred to slightly modify the terms and adapt the definitions with respect to the last two senses in the chart, so that they would better fit with my clients' experiences. I have renamed these two senses as:

▶ A Sense of Determination and;

▶ A Sense of Competency.

Statistics

To begin with, this program has proved its worth in the United States: one study covering a span of five years was carried out in schools in order to counteract the deplorable conditions found there, related to social behavior and academic performance.

Here, in brief, are some of the data from the program's official results:

a) A noticeable **decrease** in acts of vandalism;

b) A **decrease** in drop-out rates from 16% to 4%;

c) A decrease in teacher absenteeism.

Also observed was:

a) A general **increase** in the school's academic results;

b) An **increase** in student attendance, reaching 99%;

c) An **increase** in university attendance from 65% to 89%.

These compelling and enviable results demonstrate that such a program deserves to be widely implemented for the benefit of children and teachers alike.

Description of the Five Senses

It is important to properly describe each of the Five Senses that form the basis of self-esteem, as we will use them later on in exercises in order to evaluate and improve each of them.

A SENSE OF SECURITY

This represents a sense of well-being, of confidence that you feel in certain circumstances or in relation to certain projects. In contrast, there is feeling worried, being afraid or harboring doubts, which can apply regardless of our age.

For children, establishing regularity, a certain routine in their lifestyle, can increase this feeling. Clear and consistent rules will contribute to making them feel secure.

As for adults, this sense can be reflected in the social, emotional, financial or professional spheres. You will promote your sense of security by taking true responsibility for your life, making conscious choices, using your time wisely and acting on your areas of influence in order to better manage your life, while accepting the things over which you have no power.

A SENSE OF IDENTITY

This feeling is related to your self-knowledge. Once again, it refers to a realistic image of yourself, and the value that you grant yourself. It's about accepting who you are, capitalizing on your strengths and respecting your limits.

By living consciously, you will be able to clearly define your expectations in life and save yourself from the pangs of burnout, which almost always occurs when you fail to meet other people's expectations.

During my workshops or in potential assessment interviews, I invariably ask the candidates to name three of their qualities; I am amazed that the majority of people find this so difficult; some barely succeed and often find it easier to define their faults. For many, if they have to verbalize their qualities in front of several people, it takes tremendous effort and often causes embarrassment. For some, it is sheer torture.

A SENSE OF BELONGING

This is the feeling of satisfaction you get from being part of a group, large or small: with the family, at school, at work, in a team, etc., and with which you maintain a bond. This also includes the roles you take on within these groups.

Normally, we feel a certain pride in being associated with a particular group; otherwise our sense of belonging deteriorates, affecting our self-esteem. You can attribute greater personal value to yourself because you are part of *this* family or *that* private club. In the business world, we often talk about a *sense of belonging* to define this feeling.

For example, in sports, people often work as a team, which fosters a strong sense of belonging. The same applies for certain companies where employees take great pride in saying that they are employed by *this* or *that* company, giving them the impression that this increases their self-worth.

In adolescence, this need develops significantly, revolving around friends and peers, sometimes even to the detriment of the family. In order to be accepted, young people will adopt a specific dress code and behaviors according to the type of group they belong to. This is a crucial stage in their development and despite signs of rebellious independence, these young people need support from the adults who are close to them.

To foster this feeling, it is beneficial to be more open to others and to remain vigilant in maintaining healthy relationships. Be a "happy camper" by trying to improve your family and work environments: do not hesitate to express your appreciation and support to those around you; it builds closer ties.

A SENSE OF DETERMINATION

This is defined as your ability to set realistic goals for yourself and the courage to reach them by empowering yourself to achieve them. Determination and perseverance are the twin factors you necessarily need to accomplish your goals.

Setting goals is a skill that can easily be foster in children, as well as adults, even if it is something they are not used to. However, the energy needed to invest in thinking and acting according to our goals, despite obstacles or fears, remains more difficult to develop, especially in our current society where instant gratification is our way of life.

I have met many people from my client base who showed courage and a fierce determination to fight for survival, even though their other four senses had almost shrunk into oblivion due to the circumstances they had lived through. It was from this sense of determination that they were able to rebuild their self-esteem.

To keep this sense active, feel free to step out of your *comfort zone* and seek out new challenges. To do this, you may need to scrutinize your beliefs about failure, and of course, set goals and invest yourself in achieving them.

A SENSE OF COMPETENCY

The sense of competency is the *awareness* of your abilities. In general, competency refers to your abilities and your knowledge; in fact, it refers to all of your achievements. It can also include the propensity to make the right decisions at the right time.

All of the roles that we play in life, spouse, parent, workers, friends, etc., in some way, make us evaluate ourselves. Am I a competent parent? Am I a reliable friend? And so on.

To develop this sense: first, be the best you can be, nothing more! Know how to invest in your continued growth, without setting limits.

Self-Esteem:
A Precious Flower

Let us imagine the Five Senses of Self-Esteem as petals, forming a precious flower.

What do you do next with this flower? What does it need to thrive? I can hear your various answers: water, sunlight, vitamins. In short, attentive and diligent care is the answer. How many plants have withered and died, or been drowned, by a lack of experienced care?

The same goes for your own, precious self-esteem. When was the last time you took care of it? What will you do if it shows signs of distress? If it fades? If it is attacked by all kinds of environmental factors?

Squalls in the Workplace

On a related note, what happens when strong gusts of wind hit you in the workplace? The loss of a job can make someone unproductive, and turn them into somewhat of a "nobody," since socially, they can no longer define themselves, or answer that million-dollar question, "What do you do for a living?" This embarrassing situation can negatively affect this person's dignity.

To illustrate the point, let's look at two difficult cases that occurred within the work environment.

Michael and His Demotion

Michael has been a foreman at a manufacturing company for over twelve years. One day he is called into the boss's office for a brief evaluation and told that he doesn't cut it as a foreman anymore and that he will be transferred to administration. He reacts badly to the situation, for it is a sudden shock, as surprising as a heart attack would be.

As one might expect, this massive shock shattered his sense of identity. First, came the self-doubt, then the revolt, and then these questions started assailing him: "It may be true…". "After all, have I even been a good foreman all these years…? Who knows, they might just be right…". Many other questions whirled through his head, making him question his sense of competency at work.

A series of private consultations with me helped him to understand the impact this situation had on his self-esteem and make him aware of the political issues involved. Moreover, Michael realized that his identity was not solely based on his professional skills and that he also had other great personal qualities. He was able to relearn how to value himself as well as have a better opinion of himself. This experience taught him a lot and gave him better balance in his life. Since then, he has invested his energy in several areas, and not only in his work.

Pierre and the Brutal Firing

Pierre holds a management position in a distribution company. One day, his boss asks him to attend a training session and gives him the address where it will take place.

He shows up on the scheduled day and time, yet strangely, the place in question is actually a business office. In the presence of the company president, he is told of his firing, effective immediately, despite his twenty-five years of loyal service. He is instructed not to go back to his company; his personal effects will be mailed to his home address. Of course, he is offered financial compensation and a reassignment program, which meant about fifteen hours of consultation with me.

When such an ordeal befalls someone, it is like a hurricane ravaging their life! If you or someone close to you has experienced a similar situation, you know what a devastating effect it can have. In this case, each of the senses of self-esteem is affected, each petal of the flower is savagely attacked. Unfortunately, these things happen more often than you would think.

After receiving such a terrible blow, it goes without saying that some people literally fall apart. Of course, it is understandable. In turn, if these individuals do not receive any support, their demotivating experience will morph into physical or mental discomfort, sometimes even leading to depression. Without question, a situation like this cuts deep, all the way to the soul, and it is more important than ever to provide care for this suffering flower.

To get back to Pierre, since he has a very high resistance to stress, he reacted to this disaster much better than the average person. Once he got over the shock, he was able to keep his spirits up, and in a few months, he managed to land a new job in the same industry thanks to a solid network of contacts. It could have been much more dramatic had he not found another position so quickly.

During this time, I supported him and provided him with certain tools that he could use to eliminate his anger and all of the emotions linked to his feelings of revolt. However, Pierre was more affected by the repercussions on his family that were brought about by the loss of his job. At first, he felt responsible for his wife's reaction, as she fell ill due to the insecurity of the situation. Circumstances forced him to learn how to better manage this discomfort. Then he felt like less of a father because his budget cutback no longer allowed him to spoil his son as he had before. As a result, he took this opportunity to reassess some of his fundamental values.

Diminishing Situations

You might have experienced less tragic, but equally devaluing situations at work that affected your self-esteem, whether it was:

- A transfer you considered unfair;
- A discouraging evaluation;
- A sudden change in your work team;
- A patronizing or aggressive boss;
- A manipulative colleague;
- A failed project;
- Other devaluing situations.

Which of your senses was most affected? Your sense of security? Your sense of identity? Your sense of belonging? Determination? Competency? How did you deal with it? Did you consult someone to help you get rid of your negative emotions and get a fresh start?

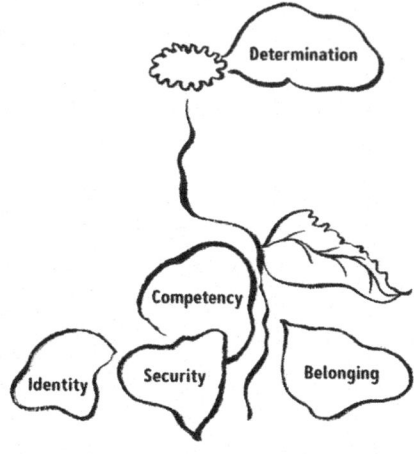

Windy Weather
and Our Self-Esteem Flower

We have just seen examples from the workplace, but the same phenomenon can occur for any of life's storms, and in turn, one or more of your senses may be affected by these challenges.

Clearly, any major, or even minor, negative event can blow over your flower and have a definite impact on one or more of its petals.

If you have ever been through a divorce, bereavement, bankruptcy, failure, retirement, or made the decision to stay home for your children: What happened to your sense of identity? Security? Belonging? Determination? Competency? Which one was most affected by the situation? Which one have you been able to bank on to rebuild yourself?

Self-Esteem and Survival

Is self-esteem a fad? A trend? Or is it an essential tool for the future?

First, it should be noted that this concept has existed for a very long time in psychology. As early as 1891, William James, an American psychologist, established, "the absence of a direct link between a person's objective qualities and the degree of satisfaction that he has with himself[10]". It was only near the end of the 1980s that significant research was carried out on the subject. Afterwards, the concept was greatly refined and became increasingly popular among individuals as well as in the clinical environment.

In his universal and essential needs pyramid, Abraham Maslow placed self-esteem in fourth position in his Hierarchy of Needs, giving priority to vital needs, followed by the need for security, then the need to love and be loved. The most fundamental of needs was situated at the top of the pyramid: the need for self-realization.

---

10 André, Christophe and Lelord, François (2007), Self-Esteem, Liking Yourself in Order to Live Better with Others.

Along with the studies carried out on this subject, society has also evolved since then and has reached a certain level of maturity. Today, we no longer have to struggle to survive as our forefathers did in the colonial period. The basic needs of the majority are now a given, and there are social programs to address any existing discrepancies in meeting the need for security. People's consciousness has become more and more enlightened, to the point that our society realizes the importance or acquiring self-esteem and self-realization.

As we have said, our social constructs have changed (family, marriage, authority, etc.). We have to rebuild our identity and re-establish our self-worth, both as a society and as individuals.

Thus, we can consider self-esteem as the basic, essential equipment for this expedition through modern life in which we are participating.

Ready to get to work? On your mark, get set... Go!

CHAPTER 3

ORIENTING OR ASSESSING YOUR LEVEL OF SELF-ESTEEM

∼

When you find that you have lost your way
and you are unable to determine
which direction to choose,
stop and try to take stock:

- *Where am I?*

- *Where am I going?*

- *Where are the headwinds?*[11]

∼

---

11 Descheneaux, Jean-Georges (1990). *Guide pratique de survie en forêt Canadienne.*
(A Practical Survival Guide in Canadian Forests), p.33.

Orienting Yourself

Notes to the Reader

This section presents several exercises to help you to situate your overall level of self-esteem. I call this global assessment: GPS / MY SELF-ESTEEM BALANCE SHEET.

You can assess your self-esteem by completing the table: GPS / MY SELF-ESTEEM BALANCE SHEET at the end of this section, by proceeding as you wish in either those two ways:

1. By the systematic method: that I propose to you by the following directions throughout this section. At the end of each exercise, you report the positive or negative balance in the appropriate column in the GPS / MY SELF-ESTEEM BALANCE SHEET at the end of the section. You will make the final calculation after completing the set of exercises in your expedition journal.

2. By the spontaneous method: if you wish to assess your level of self-esteem without doing the suggested exercises, go straight to the compilation table: GPS / MY SELF-ESTEEM BALANCE SHEET. Answer each element intuitively by marking a "plus (+)" or a "minus (-)" depending on the positive (+) or negative (-) perception you have for that point. However, if you choose this method, your results are more likely to be biased because you will not know the definitions of the key elements, or because your self-perception in general is unrealistic.

Knowing Where You Are

Orienting Yourself During an Expedition

No matter what type of expedition you are on, if at some point you get lost, whether you are on a boat, in a plane, car, on a bicycle or even on foot, you will undoubtedly have to ask yourself the following questions: — *Where am I? — Where am I going? — What are the headwinds?*

In fact, to reach your destination, it would be desirable for you to learn how to orient yourself in order to be able to find your way back, if necessary. Moreover, being familiar with these two instruments in particular is necessary to know how to orient yourself in nature: the compass and the typographic map.

Orienting Yourself in Life

The same goes for your personal life, when you feel like you no longer know where you are and are unable to determine the direction you should choose, *stop and try to take stock* of what is going on in your life.

Here, you also have two essential tools to find your way. Your compass is your self-esteem, and the road map translates into a list of your life goals or aspirations.

Have no fear, even if you are convinced that you do not know how to use your self-esteem and your life goals to your advantage at this time, together, we will see how over the next few chapters.

You can therefore answer the first question, "*Where am I?*" by assessing the level of your self-esteem (GPS / My Self-Esteem Balance Sheet). As you go through

> *Self-esteem is our compass, and our list of life goals, our road map!*

this section, you will also be able to identify some obstacles (headwinds) that cause your low self-esteem or that prevent from improving it.

In chapter 4, there are *three valuable lists* that you will have to complete, and which will no doubt allow you to clearly determine the direction you wish to pursue (*Where am I going?*)

Our Internal Compass

Self-esteem is a constant and dynamic part of your life, without necessarily being the key to everything that you do. It is, however, a very good indicator and can even become a catalyst to move you towards your life goals, to the extent that you believe you deserve them. But beware; there is a catch! Self-esteem can also be a drag, because low self-esteem can undoubtedly prevent you from setting goals.

Just like a compass that points to the magnetic north and helps you to find yourself, a healthy self-esteem allows you to chart your life's path, or to find it again if you are lost.

Elizabeth comes from a large family and will soon be 50 years old. She works as a clerk in a store. Until now, luck has not smiled upon her, however, we hear her regularly say: "*I don't want anything more in my life, I have my house, I am satisfied.*" However, since she has been experiencing significant financial difficulties which are negatively affecting her relationship with her significant other, she might want more in terms of her budget.

In our discussions together, she identified two deep beliefs that have inevitably hindered her personal and professional development and which she phrased as: "*I don't deserve more in life*" and "*It's better to be satisfied with what one has so as not to be disappointed.*" This way of thinking does not motivate her to carry out other projects. As we can see, her hope of improving herself is completely inhibited by her poor self-esteem.

Life's Seasons

Many parts of North America enjoy four seasons annually. The same phenomenon can be observed in our own lives. In fact, we cycle through spring, summer, fall and winter. Such is life!

In his book *The Seasons of Success*,[12] Denis Waitley describes them as follows:

- Winter: The season for dreaming and planning;
- Spring: The season for planting;
- Summer: The season for growing and cultivating;
- Fall: The season for harvesting and dispersing.

---

12 Waitley, Denis, E. (1986). Seasons of Success, now in audiobook format.

However, the distinction between the seasons of life and the calendar seasons must be understood; they do not necessarily correspond. They are not all of identical duration; for example, the season in which you plan your goals (winter) may be very short—a few weeks at most may be sufficient—while the planting season (spring) can sometimes extend for months or even years.

Seasons always come at certain times of the year, in a specific order that we fortunately, or unfortunately, cannot control. They are inexorably linked and we can only reap what we have sown. If we draw a parallel, so do the seasons of success, which repeat themselves constantly and indefinitely: that is why we cannot be successful "once and for all."

What is interesting to realize, however, is that you may find yourself in a different season of success in each of the different areas in your life: in love, you may be at the springtime of a relationship, while professionally, you are maybe reaping the fruits of your labors.

The same goes for your self-esteem. Depending on the severity or mildness of each season, your self-esteem will be affected either negatively or positively. There are times when you will need to think and do more inner work, while at others, you will effortlessly enjoy the sense of your self-worth.

GPS / In the Field

These days, people are familiar with GPS (Global Positioning System) from car or cell phone use.

Invented by the American government at the end of 70s, here's a quick reminder of how it works. A GPS is a pocket satellite navigation device that provides data allowing you to know your exact geographical location at all times. With this information, you can adjust your course as needed, in order to reach your destination.

GPS / Self-Esteem

In psychology, the GPS method from *Genèse de perception de soi*[13], (in English, *Genesis of Self Concept*), is used to describe and explain the elements that make up who we are, at the moment of self-analysis.

---

13 L'Écuyer, René (1990). Méthodologie de l'analyse développementale de contenu : Méthode GPS et concept de soi. (Methodology of developmental content analysis: GPS method and self-concept).

Furthering this analogy, I have combined the two definitions, one from the navigation device and one from psychology, to create the concept of GPS / SELF-ESTEEM. I encourage you to use it in the sense of *the state or position of my self-esteem in the current moment.* As self-esteem fluctuates depending on the phase you are in, or what life events are happening, you can re-evaluate it at any time.

The Position
of Your Self-Esteem

After having read these first chapters that have helped you to better understand the basics of self-esteem, now is the time to assess your current self-esteem position (GPS).

As you read this guide, you might have taken notes or had some spontaneous reactions that prompted you to assess your own self-esteem. This is a good reflex! But I would like to take you a step further in developing your self-esteem, and for that, you need to have a clear picture of the real position of your self-esteem. I therefore suggest a balance sheet, using an accounting formula with two columns (+ and -). Do not worry though, you will be the only one to check the content.

This balance sheet, this simple, basic tool, becomes a GPS / ESTEEM because it determines where you stand, and can tell you in which areas you will have to invest in order to improve your self-esteem, your self-worth.

Primary Instructions For Performing All The Exercises And Completing The Table "Gps / My Self-Esteem Balance Sheet" (at the end of this section)

---

1. Use your EXPEDITION JOURNAL for all exercises. You can reproduce the BALANCE SHEET for personal use, and thus be able to compare your progress when you repeat these exercises.

2. Be kind to yourself, that is, neither overly critical nor overly tolerant, as you probably would be when giving your honest opinion to a friend.

3. Do each exercise with the goal of continually improving and not as an exercise to make you feel guilty or depressed.

4. Keep this data to yourself; no one needs to analyze your assessment!

5. There are no *right* or *wrong answers* per se. *Your*s is the right one.

6. Use the table to rate each item. Enter a plus sign (+) in the corresponding column if you judge that your self-esteem is positive in relation to the element in question; otherwise, enter a minus sign (-) if you feel that your self-esteem needs improving.

7. You will be given other information after each exercise to help you compile all of your answers.

EXERCISE # 1   THE STRENGTH OF YOUR SELF-ESTEEM

To help you assess the strength of your self-esteem, we will use the following table indicating the four types of self-esteem developed by Drs. André and Lelord in their book "Self-Esteem, Liking Yourself in Order to Live Better With Others[14]".

Take a close look at the table first. There are four types of self-esteem there; for each, a general reaction is described in relation to a key situation, a success, a compliment, a failure and a criticism.

TYPES OF SELF-ESTEEM	MY TYPICAL REACTION TO SUCCESS	MY TYPICAL REACTION TO A COMPLIMENT	MY TYPICAL REACTION TO FAILURE	MY TYPICAL REACTION TO A CRITIQUE
HIGH & STABLE SELF-ESTEEM	"I am happy, it made me happy to have done it..."	"Thank you very much."	"I didn't succeed this time."	"All right, ... and why are you telling me this?"
HIGH & UNSTABLE SELF-ESTEEM	"I told you so, and wait for it, you haven't seen anything yet; those who didn't believe me then don't look very bright today."	"More, more!"	"What do you know about it in the first place?"	"And you, have you looked at yourself lately?"
LOW & UNSTABLE SELF-ESTEEM	"Am I going to be up to it now?"	"Oh, you know, I don't deserve any credit."	"I had problems preparing, I wasn't good."	"You think so?"
LOW & STABLE SELF-ESTEEM	Falls seriously ill eight days after	"Stop it, that doesn't interest me."	"Yes, I am stupid, you hadn't realized that yet?"	"Yes, and even more than you're thinking."

---

14 André, Christophe and Lelord, François (2007). Self-Esteem, Liking Yourself in Order to Live Better with Others.

Under each typical reaction, find the answer that applies to you most often, and then read the summary analysis corresponding to your type of self-esteem. In the conclusion, you will be able to locate the symbols (+) or (-), representing the result of your reactions to the four given situations, to be reported on the GPS / MY SELF-ESTEEM BALANCE SHEET

Summary Analysis

A *high and stable self-esteem* is strong and resistant. You are not inclined to constantly question yourself. Setbacks do not make you feel inferior.

A *high and unstable self-esteem* makes you vulnerable. You have a tendency to take any challenge very seriously, as if your life depends on it.

A *low and unstable self-esteem* makes you very "sensitive and reactive to external events, whether positive or negative." Your self-worth increases and decreases regularly. Your image is very important to you, and you aim to please.

A *low and stable self-esteem* makes you look down on yourself. You may feel resigned to your fate and tend to see the negative side of things.

Conclusions Regarding the Strength of your Esteem

For each of the four preceding situations, record the result (+) or (-) in your expedition journal, depending on your answer:

☐ *I have a high and stable self-esteem*: positive on the BALANCE sheet (+).

☐ *I have a high and unstable self-esteem*: negative on the BALANCE sheet (-).

☐ *I have a low and unstable self-esteem*: negative on the BALANCE sheet (-).

☐ *I have a low and stable self-esteem*: negative on the BALANCE sheet (-).

Transcribe it in your journal in the table GPS / MY SELF-ESTEEM BALANCE SHEET, EXERCISE #1.

EXERCISE # 2   YOUR SELF-ESTEEM THERMOMETER

On a slightly lighter note, here is a Self-Esteem Thermometer, graduated from 0 to 100 degrees Celsius, on which statements are written. Look on the thermometer for the statement (s) that characterize you the most often at this point in time. You can react on the spot, or observe yourself for a few days and write down what you say most frequently: "I must" or "I choose," etc.

This exercise can be done to evaluate your life globally, or for each of the areas of your life that you specifically want to assess.

Of course, this exercise is by no means scientific, but it has the advantage of being able to quickly identify some of the most common behaviors that you may adopt in your life. I therefore suggest that you *periodically* take note of your *self-esteem temperature* in your journal:

1. Firstly, to realize where you are at;

2. Then as a benchmark to improve yourself, and also;

3. To be aware of your progress when you redo that exercise at a later date.

SELF-ESTEEM THERMOMETER

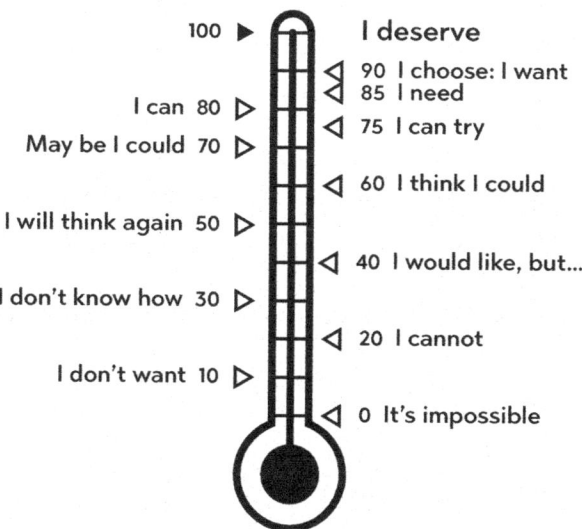

If you find it difficult to situate yourself on your own, you can validate your answers that are most relevant to who you are, with someone who knows you well AND whom you trust completely. This validation can also strengthen your point of view.

Summary Analysis

At 100 °C: You believe that you deserve the good and beautiful things in life!

From 75 ° to 90 °C: Indicates increasingly open attitudes where you make room for determination and assertion of your needs and personal choices.

From 60 ° to 75 °C: You are gaining more confidence, persevere in this direction, you have everything to gain.

From 30 ° to 60 °C: This gradation describes behaviors tinged with a lack of confidence and hesitation in your actions, despite a glimmer of hope that things will improve. Dare to take your place.

From 0 ° to 30 °C: Your way of talking suggests that you are skilled in the art of "self-sabotage". Know that self-esteem requires you to take responsibility for your life.

Conclusions Regarding Your Self-Esteem Thermometer

Situate yourself on the Self-Esteem Thermometer and, depending on your answer, record the result of a (+) or a (-) in your journal in the table GPS / MY SELF-ESTEEM BALANCE SHEET, EXERCISE #2.

☐ *I am over 60 degrees C*: positive on the BALANCE SHEET (+).

☐ *I am less than 60 degrees C*: negative on the BALANCE SHEET (-).

EXERCISE # 3   YOUR SELF-ESTEEM PER LIFE SPHERE

Here is another way to determine your level of self-esteem. Think of it in terms of each area of your life. What rating do you give yourself for each? Which is the strongest? The weakest?

First, give yourself a rating from one to five, for each of the following spheres:

➤ 1 if you think you have *low* self-esteem and

➤ 5 if you think you have a *high* self-esteem.

Life sphere	From 1 to 5	+	–
Family			
Financial			
Physical			
Romantic relationships			
Social			
Professional / work			

Then, in the two other columns, for each aspect of your life, mark:

➤ a minus (-) if you marked a 1, 2 or 3.

➤ a plus (+) if you marked a 4 or 5.

Summary Analysis

1) The higher your rating; the stronger the feeling of self-worth you have in that sphere of life.

2) Particularly note the life sphere in which you gave yourself the highest rating. Does this reflect the area where you are most comfortable? The happiest?

3) What is the sphere in which you got the lowest rating? Does it correspond to the area of your life where you are most vulnerable? Where you have the most difficulty? Do not hesitate to invest the necessary energy to perfect that sphere.

Conclusions Regarding Your Self-Esteem per Life Sphere

Record your answer (+ or -) for each sphere in your journal in the table GPS / MY SELF-ESTEEM BALANCE SHEET, EXERCISE #3.

Position Yourself According to the Five Senses

Here, you can review the details of each sense that forms the basis of self-esteem (senses of self-esteem as described earlier in the previous chapter), with real-life examples. For each one, ask yourself questions and evaluate yourself. You will also find comments on the risks incurred if this sense is underdeveloped. Here are the Five Senses of Self-Esteem:

The five senses of self-esteem:

- A Sense of Identity;
- A Sense of Determination;
- A Sense of Belonging;
- A Sense of Security;
- A Sense of Competence.

SENSE OF IDENTITY

The sense of identity allows you to be aware of your strengths and abilities, but also your limits. Of course, this self-image should be as realistic as possible.

In addition to knowing yourself *well*, the sense of identity involves self-acceptance of your potential and who you are. This does not mean that you don't have anything to improve; on the contrary, having a clear picture of yourself can only be beneficial.

Identity and behavior

Nowadays, the current values conveyed by our industrialized society favor people's identity based on what they *do*, in terms of performance or concrete achievements, and not by virtue of *who* they are as human beings.

With the changing economy, are you allowing yourself to fully achieve your own goals and aspirations in relation to your career? Or are you inclined to mold yourself to the demands of the market to determine your career choice?

Does your standard of living meet your fundamental needs, or rather the lifestyle advocated by society's standards? How many people would like to extend their parental leave, but cannot because their financial obligations are preventing them?

As an educator or as a parent, to avoid this kind of identity confusion related to performance, it would be extremely valuable to teach children early on to listen to themselves and to respect them in their self-discovery. Thus, in adolescence, their choices would certainly be less heartbreaking if they are already used to knowing and trusting themselves.

There is another educational attitude that can help reduce the risks associated with identity problems, and that is making children realize the difference between their behaviors and their identity. In an upsetting situation, why not tell them something like "I don't appreciate what you just did but I love you..." or "I love you for who you are, and not for what you do..."?

Even adults are surprised to hear these types of comments coming from a friend or a spouse. When these constructive remarks are made, it is the ultimate recognition of who you are as a *unique* human being.

Keep in mind that you are so much more than what you do or produce!

WHAT "I AM NOT"

I am not my will, it changes in intensity.

I am not my emotions, they go through me.

I am not my thoughts, they are constantly changing.

I am not my body which changes with the passing of time.

I am not my actions, nor my successes nor my failures.

I am!

Suzan, confided in me that a rather dramatic event allowed her to realize who she was deep down, and even spiritually. She said that one day, her ex-partner got angry and violently pushed her; she got stuck in the closet and he kept the door shut tight. She said to me: "Even though I was screaming with all my might, it was as if I was pulling away from myself and the situation at the same time; my gut was telling me that he could never reach my 'true self.' It gave me strength, and that day was the last time he ever set foot in the house. I had finally put my finger on my real identity, this 'me' that I never knew was there!"

To complement this example, I would add a few lines concerning abused women. In the majority of cases of violence, it is obvious that the victim's self-esteem is at its lowest. Often the aggressor ends up convincing the victim that she deserved the beatings because she had provoked him. It becomes very complicated in the mind of the assaulted person, they no longer have their own identity and start to believe that *they deserve to be punished.*

If I can express one wish for victims of physical or psychological violence, it is that they can get help in order to regain their identity as well as regain some control over their life; whether through individual consultations or self-esteem workshops.

The Risks Related to a Weak Sense of Identity

Failure to give yourself a realistic sense of self-worth, whether it be under-valued or overvalued, incurs the risk of straying too far from your life's path, from your personal destination, because your compass is out of whack.

Your mistaken beliefs, which have been conditioned by your experiences, may alter reality, or the true value of your sense of identity. Sometimes, a close reevaluation is necessary to fairly re-establish your beliefs and allow you to have a more realistic sense of who you are. Otherwise, other people will always hold more value to you than yourself.

Moreover, if you value so little of yourself, you will seek value it in the approving gaze of others, which can only lead to problematic self-esteem patterns, as demonstrated by the following example. Perhaps this story is similar to yours, or that of a friend.

Dennis is an "eternal" student, accumulating diplomas to gain recognition from his parents, recognition that never comes. He is almost forty years old, with a collection of science and management degrees in his drawers: a degree in law is his last chance to prove himself. When he finally gets his license to practice, his mother simply says to him: "We knew you would." She says nothing more, no emotional recognition of his efforts or for all his other successes, no appreciation. The emotional drought helps banish him to his inner desert.

EXERCICE # 4   GPS / IDENTITY

The following is a questionnaire on your sense of identity, the results of which you should record in your journal in your overall balance sheet (GPS / MY SELF-ESTEEM BALANCE SHEET). Respond with yes or no answers.

1. Do I sometimes feel that I am only exploiting a small fraction of my talents?

2. Do I hesitate to do things for fear of failure?

3. Am I used to put myself in problematic situations?

4. Am I very preoccupied with what other people think of me?

5. How often do I doubt my abilities?

6. Do others see me as better than what I think I am?

7. Am I often anxious and struggling with feelings of guilt?

8. How often do I feel depressed?

9. Do I have trouble taking care of myself?

10. Do I feel that others do not sufficiently recognize my efforts or my merits?

11. Do I think that I am "unlovable" (means "Can anyone really love me ... me?")?

12. Am I a regular burnout candidate?

TOTAL: _____ / 12

Add up all of the responses where you answered YES.

Summary Analysis

1. The more times you answered *yes*, the more your self-esteem related to your sense of identity needs to be strengthened and nurtured. This sense is one of the most important among the five senses that make up your core self-esteem, your own self-worth. Do not neglect it.

2. Pay special attention to questions 11 and 12, which are crucial indications of your sense of identity. If you have answered *yes* to either of these questions, feel free to invest the required energy to uncover the root causes behind this belief and health condition.

3. Make a note of the other items to which you answered *yes*; this tells you what you can focus on in your work to develop a stronger sense of identity.

Conclusions Regarding Your Sense of Identity

If you have 5 YESES or less, your sense of identity is relatively strong: add a positive on the balance sheet (+).

If you have 6 YESES or more, your sense of identity shows a certain weakness: add a negative on the balance sheet (-).

Record it in your journal in the table GPS / MY SELF-ESTEEM BALANCE SHEET, EXERCISE #4.

YOUR DIGNITY

The sense of identity is intimately linked to the dignity that you recognize within yourself as a human being. Dignity relates to *self-love*, your self-respect. In this sense, dignity is a very interesting indicator to assess in establishing your self-esteem balance sheet.

Here are some thoughts on your dignity. At this point in my life, do I feel that:

- I am trustworthy?
- I am worthy to receive?
- I am worthy of love, or in other words: Can anyone really love me?
- I am worthy of respect?
- Do I deserve to be respected?
- I am worthy of living? Of existing?
- Do I deserve to have my own "secret garden", to keep my own intimate thoughts that I do not have to share with anyone?

EXERCICE #5   **GPS / DIGNITY**

You can compile the results to establish your GPS / DIGNITY and then record it in the overall balance sheet.

Factors Which Harm Dignity

Without making an exhaustive list of everything that can harm a person's dignity, here are a few of the more important factors. You can read this list by asking yourself the two following questions:

Are any of these factors a part of your life? If so, do you feel that the factor in question affects your dignity?

☐ A lack of respect (words, violence, unjustified firing, etc.;)

☐ Isolation;

☐ Violence;

☐ Poverty;

☐ Incompetence;

☐ Obsession over performance;

☐ Instability: family or financial;

☐ Religious fundamentalism;

☐ Racism;

☐ Others.

Conclusions Regarding Your Dignity

☐ If you did not tick off any items, your sense of dignity reflects your self-esteem: put a positive on the balance sheet (+).

☐ If you have ticked off ONE or more of these elements, your sense of dignity is undoubtedly affected: put a negative on the balance sheet (-).

Record your result in your journal on the table GPS / MY SELF-ESTEEM BALANCE SHEET, EXERCISE #5

YOUR SENSE OF SECURITY

The sense of security refers to your confidence in getting whatever it takes to meet your needs, whether emotionally, materially or financially; it is also linked to your ability to take risks.

Economically, probably due to globalization and the major changes in the management of companies, we hear more and more people saying—in terms of employment or career—that "Security does not exist anymore". Even if we keep repeating it on a large scale, it is hardly reassuring. Also, it would be good to see how each person experiences this disturbing reality. Could there be a cause and effect link between this state of affairs and the growing number of illnesses related to psychological disorders? These are very appropriate questions for further research.

In a documentary, I had the opportunity to see a **family of circus trapeze artist**s who, for four generations, have made a living from this *activity that can certainly be described as very dangerous*. In fact, several family members had died from fatal accidents at work: a father, a grandfather, etc., and yet, the family continues to introduce their young ones to this profession. This is how we developed the attitude of mastering our fears and walking a tightrope despite the risks.

Thus, security is sometimes a question of perception.

Insecurity

The level of stress related to insecurity is unique to each person. The tendency to worry, above all, can be a personality trait. However, other factors may also influence it, such as your family history or your own experiences. If you demonstrate a good ability to deal with stress, it will allow you to move much more smoothly through the turbulent areas of your life.

If you come from a very anxious family where no one took risks, then it can be difficult for you to take risks on your own. This applies in all areas, emotional or material.

Anne-Marie is self-employed and comes from a family that has constantly lived in financial insecurity due to her father never having stable work. She has grown used to this lifestyle and has become so resistant to this kind of stress that she feels no financial worries, even though she is virtually penniless.

On the other hand, **Chantal** is a businesswoman who is very comfortable from a material point of view; she has a very large financial portfolio. However, she regularly feels worried about money issues, without being able to explain this feeling that she has always lived with.

As a counselor, I saw a number of clients who said they could not leave their job, despite the suffocating, even unbearable circumstances, "because they had to earn a living", due to their multiple responsibilities: children, a house, financial commitments. Here is a concrete example to illustrate my point.

Claude was one of those people who said he could not quit his job even though he was utterly unhappy with the direction his career was taking. Furious with his situation, he continued to accumulate problems, but according to him, there was nothing he could do about it, even if he changed jobs. He kept saying that he "couldn't afford a 90-degree turn because he had to make a living and meet his financial responsibilities".

Claude and his wife were among those who aimed to pay off their mortgage as quickly as possible, but given their situation, they were making things a lot harder than they needed to be. After much discussion, they came to a solution of simply reducing their monthly payments so that they could breathe easier. Claude was then able to spend time reflecting in order to reorient his career.

Revising your priorities in life while navigating a storm can be greatly beneficial and allow you to go back to school, or to simply give you leisure time to take care of yourself, the time to change the situation in question.

For years, some people will endure and suffer the devastating effects of a deplorable marital situation, a demoralizing job or belittling relationships, without seeing any possible way out, paralyzed by the fear of the unknown. What about you?

Risks Associated With a Weak Sense of Security

A lack of emotional security can lead to relying more on others than on oneself, in order to nurture this lack of consideration and affection; we risk becoming emotionally dependent. Deficiencies in this sense can cause major problems in your interpersonal relationships, especially your romantic ones.

If you draw your sense of security externally instead of internally, you will inevitably become dependent on it. You will hang on to it.

What will happen once this person or this activity lets go or ends??? Once again, you will have the feeling that "you were not really worth it" and that deep belief "you deserve to be rejected."

Because of a lack of internal security, you can end up constantly doubting your choices, your decisions, and give more weight to the opinions of others rather than your own. Thus, you worship them in recognition. You find them to be "better than yourself" and the vicious cycle sets in, you judge yourself to be "less good," and your self-confidence and self-esteem declines.

EXERCISE # 6   GPS / SECURITY

The following is a questionnaire to situate your sense of security at this point in time. Answer with a *yes* or a *no*.

Points given for a "yes"

1. Am I often afraid of being rejected?   -1
2. Do I often endure unpleasant situations for fear
   of *losing* someone or something?   -1
3. Am I naturally worried about anything and everything?   -1
4. Am I inclined to trust the opinions of others over mine?   -1
5. Am I ambivalent when I have to make important decisions?   -1
6. Do I remain confident most of the time after making decisions?   2
7. Do I trust my own judgment?   2
8. Am I able to take risks?   2
9. Do I deserve to love?   2
10. Do I deserve to be loved?   2

For each *yes*, assign the corresponding score
and add them up.   **TOTAL:** _____

Summary Analysis

1. The closer the score is to 10, the more your sense of security seems to be developed and stable.

2. If you have answered *yes* to question 2, explore why this fear of losing someone or something prevent you from taking risks, even calculated ones.

3. Pay special attention to questions 9 and 10, especially if you answered *no*. It would probably be wise to work on these vital elements for your personal balance.

4. Write down the items to which you answered *yes* for questions 1 to 5 inclusively, as well as the ones to which you answered *no* for questions 6 to 10. They indicate precisely what you have to consider in order to improve your sense of security.

Conclusions Regarding Your Sense of Security

☐ If you scored a 6 or higher: that's a positive balance (+).

☐ If you scored a 5 or less: that's a negative balance (-).

Record your results in your journal in the table GPS / MY SELF-ESTEEM BALANCE SHEET, EXERCISE #6.

YOUR SENSE OF BELONGING

This pride in being part of a group allows you to feel worthy in your own eyes and often in those of others: whether it is the company you work for, a political group, a social or religious group to which you belong, a sports team or a family of which you are proud to be a part.

Indeed, studies have shown that the heart, and even the body, heal much better and more quickly in a supportive living environment[15].

I will therefore address here the topic of divorce which, by itself, seriously affects the sense of belonging for all those involved, either directly or indirectly; we are talking about the divorce itself, but also about the children, grandparents, parents and friends that often find themselves torn apart.

Most divorces cause automatic, painful cuts, when the ties with the ex-family are deep. Understandably, few divorced couples succeed to keep ongoing ties with the ex-in-laws. This certainly causes the feeling of mourning. However, nothing is forcing you to categorically sever these ties if your heart is bounded to them. How can you find ways to respect and meet your need for connection while simultaneously respecting the needs and limitations of the others involved?

You can't turn the page on 20 years of your life as if nothing had happened, or at least we shouldn't. There is more than a chapter there; it's a whole book in itself. As far as I'm concerned, the in-laws from my first marriage have been very significant people in my life during all the years that I have been around them. I have forged a very close bond with them. They are assured of my faithful love for them, even though I'm only in contact with them a few times a year. They are the grandparents of my children and, beyond that, they are my adoptive parents, my precious friends. As a matter of fact, I still refer to them as my in-laws #1, and my new in-laws are aware that I call them my in-laws #2, which doesn't detract from the quality of the relationship that we are building now. Through it all, I have respected my sense of belonging.

---

15 Many such studies are described in the book *La Guérison du cœur (The Healing of the Heart)* by Guy Corneau (2000), pp. 65-71.

Risks Related to a Weak Sense of Belonging

One thing is sure; a weak sense of belonging to a group can end up isolating you within that group. For example, you can participate in activities or work in a company without feeling necessarily proud of it. This means it is possible that you have a hard time understanding the enthusiasm of others. What do you not like about this group? Can you make it clear what your expectations are?

In addition, a misguided sense of belonging can sometimes lead to psychological disorders, for example, if you are part of a group that tells you your reactions, your way of thinking, and your individuality is no longer relevant. If staying in such a group does not allow you to grow or affects physical or mental health: please get out!

EXERCISE # 7   **GPS / SENSE OF BELONGING**

Using the following questions, you can assess your sense of belonging at this point in time. Answer with a *yes* or a *no* in your expedition journal.

Points given for a "yes"

1. Do I feel well integrated into my family by blood? My family by marriage? Or my blended family?   1

2. Am I part of a group that I am proud to belong to?   1

3. Can I clearly state the positive aspects that   my home group brings to me (family, social, professional or other)?   1

4. Do I have one or more friends?social, professional or other)   1

5. Do I feel guilty for being a part of a particular group?   -2

6. Do I feel stifled by the beliefs or ideas of the group that I am a member of?   -2

7. Do I feel compelled to be part of a defined group?   -2

For each *yes*, assign the corresponding score and add them up.   TOTAL: _____

Summary Analysis

1. The closer the score is to 4, the stronger your sense of belonging seems.

2. Remember that living in harmony in a group affects your health, even your longevity. You have a great advantage in maintaining this sense.

3. Pay special attention to questions 5, 6 and 7. If you have answered *yes*, take this opportunity to reflect and ask yourself what is going on.

No one has the right to force you to stay where you do not want to be. Ask for help if needed.

4. Write down the items to which you have answered *no* for questions 1 to 4 inclusively, and *yes* to questions 5 to 7. They indicate what you have to consider in order to develop your sense of belonging.

Conclusions Regarding Your Sense of Belonging

☐ If your score is 2 or more: it is a positive balance (+).

☐ If your score is 1 or less: it is a negative balance (-).

Record your result in your journal in the table GPS / MY SELF-ESTEEM BALANCE SHEET, EXERCISE #7.

YOUR SENSE OF DETERMINATION

This refers to your self-confidence that leads to setting realistic goals and giving yourself the means to achieve them. For over 20 years, I have been teaching techniques for setting goals. It led me to discover that self-esteem plays a major role in our belief that we deserve to attract the good and beautiful things in life.

The very definition of determination speaks of steadfastness, daring and courage. As for the sense of determination, it includes a level of energy or life force, and I might add, a taste for life itself. It is through a sense of determination that you can rebuild yourself after life's storms, and that you can regenerate your *self-esteem flower*.

Setting goals in life gives direction and meaning to your actions. It is the *happiness vitamin*, even if some of your desires never come true. In fact, to cherish and pursue these aspirations, all of which goes hand in hand with the pleasure and energy that flows from them, is worth its weight in gold a thousand times over.

It is advisable for you to periodically review your list of goals to see if they are still relevant to you in your reality. You may want to modify them to be more in line with your personal development, especially if your level of self-esteem has improved.

Danielle is being followed by a social worker as part of a depression prevention program. Having learned about the five senses that form the basis of self-esteem, she was able to grasp the negative effect that her divorce had on each petal of her self-esteem flower. It was by recognizing herself for the courage and determination she had previously shown in recovering from serious situations that she was able to regain confidence in her own power.

Risks Related to a Weak Sense of Determination

Some authors argue that the sense of determination must be a prerequisite for self-esteem, which is true in a certain sense since it must be present in order to have the strength to act on one's self-esteem. In children, however, this sense can be developed in conjunction with the sense of competency, even while they are learning at school, socially, in sports, the arts, or other activities.

People with a lack of confidence will find it very difficult to adapt to the various stressors in their life, they will lack the energy to fight as well as the hope to resolve the obstacles that will present themselves.

If you lack confidence in yourself, you could be counted among the victims who allow themselves to be controlled by others, or by the circumstances where you give up your full powers. Ultimately, you would also be prone to depression, or even sickness, which can ultimately lead to suicide.

On the other hand, that sense of determination can be misleading and play tricks on you. If you are an energetic person, a go-getter type without a specific goal, you run the risk of going around in circles for a long time since your energy expenditure will not be channeled toward a specific destination. It can make you work tirelessly, achieving very few in terms of tangible results, even after decades of overdoing it.

Another peril awaits people with great amounts of energy but who are not focused on *their* own goals. In fact, they can even become invested in carrying out projects that belong to others. This is not harmful in and of itself, except if the individual also has a low self-esteem; then they have the ideal profile to be the ultimate slaves, excessively devoted.

Moreover, there is still the possibility of people being at risk, because of a weak sense of determination. We find a lot of people who show great courage, sometimes disguising their inner doubts that eat away at them. It could be really beneficial for them to move on instead of staying stuck in place, paralyzed. On the other hand, it becomes apparent that nothing is working, and there is a real risk of exhaustion if these doubts turn into the spurs that stimulate them into acting, to doing more. Especially if they no longer know how to stop when necessary, or they continue rushing forward headlong, without even having the privilege of savoring their results. Ironically, these people act to stifle their doubts, but unfortunately they always end up doubting their results ... it becomes an endless cycle! This is often the excessive person's lot in life!

EXERCISE # 8   GPS / DETERMINATION

After having answered the following questions, you can assess your sense of determination at this point in time. Please answer *with a yes or a no.*

1. Am I naturally confident in life?
2. Do I show courage when faced with obstacles?
3. Do I have the ability to get back on my feet *quickly enough* after a hard blow?
4. Do I generally consider myself to be determined?
5. Am I naturally optimistic?
6. Do I have the means to manage my stress?
7. Do I have goals?
8. Are they precise?
9. Are they written down?
10. Do they stimulate me? Are they close to my heart?
11. Do I have the energy to pursue my goals?
12. Do I show tenacity in achieving my projects or my dreams?
13. Am I able to please myself?
14. Am I able to stop before I burn my wings?

TOTAL OF *YES*: _____ / 14

Summary Analysis

1. The more times you answered *yes* to this series of questions, the stronger and more active your sense of determination seems.

2. If you have answered *yes* to questions 6, 13 and 14, this indicates that you are taking steps to reduce your stress level related to your activities. You show balance.

3. However, if you have answered *yes* to only those three questions (6, 13, 14), you should check to see if your lack of determination is not caused by your fear of succeeding. You seem more inclined to stay comfortably in the background rather than be proactive.

4. Write down each item to which you answered "no." They will indicate what you need to improve on to strengthen your sense of determination.

Conclusions Regarding Your Sense of Determination

☐ If you answered *yes* to 7 questions or more: it's a solid positive balance (+).

☐ If you have answered yes to 6 questions or less: it's a negative balance (-).

Record your result in your journal in the table GPS / MY SELF-ESTEEM BALANCE SHEET, EXERCISE #7.

"VICTIMITIS" OR LEARNED SENSE OF HELPLESSNESS

The term victim refers to a person who suffers from the actions of others, unfortunate events, or through their own fault. In all cases, the victim feels trapped, unable to take control; they do not take responsibility for their life in this way, and believe themselves to be helpless. We are not born with this sense; it is cultivated through our experiences.

When I talk about "victimitis", I am referring to a symptom of an unhealthy behavior that takes on varying degrees of intensity ranging from mild to acute. The purpose of the following exercise is to gauge your rate of "victimitis." Is it mild or acute?

It is evident that we all play the victim from time to time. Indeed, who has never been in pain and complained more than the intensity of the pain actually felt? We have all probably experienced a moment of exhaustion accompanied by the feeling of "poor little me," where you just want to lie down on the sofa in your pyjamas and feel sorry for yourself. Is not the myth of the man cold or man flu legendary? Does a woman not want to be rocked like a baby on days when she is struggling with PMS? Have you ever had a fairly common event occurs, but embellished it until it was something dramatic to tell your friends about?

If any of these things, or something similar, happens to you occasionally, this is normal, you are part of the *mild* category of victims. It is not a crime to be a victim ... for a few hours, as long as you are aware of it. During those times, be sure to make clear requests so that those around you can meet your expectations, the way you want them to be met.

Also, realize that it is altogether human to temporarily regress, it is even healthy. It allows you to take a step back and recharge your batteries.

Risks Related to "Victimitis"

If every day you live in the shadow of an executioner, that is actually the real crime! A crime you are perpetrating against yourself in turn kills your potential, your achievements, your dreams, your happiness and your self-esteem.

It is interesting to realize, however, that the victim plays an active role in whether or not this situation continues. Indeed, victims are not necessarily passive. They often complacently play that role, consciously or unconsciously profiting from it.

Victims who soak in their "victimitis" for a long time end up, in a way, collapsing. They extinguish within themselves any hope of success and, of course, end up reaping the results that correspond with their beliefs. As a result, other tormentors and misfortunes arrive and befall them on an ongoing basis.

The Past Is No Excuse!

Every victim has his or her own story. You may have had a very tough, or even unhappy, childhood that has left you with lasting effects. Rehashing the past will not do you any good, unless you decide to take the necessary means to heal the wounds that make you dysfunctional, in order to help you move forward afterwards.

If you do not suffer from such wounds, stop looking back and ruminating on the past: it paralyzes you in your actions and development. It is like driving a car and constantly looking in the rearview mirror instead of looking ahead, making you risk missing a curve.

You are behind the wheel of your own life; you are in control of it. You are the captain of your own ship: so go ahead!

EXERCISE # 9   **GPS / VICTIMITIS**

Does any of the following happen to me:

- ☐ Unduly endure a situation instead of managing it?
- ☐ Complain without looking for solutions?
- ☐ Know what to do to change a situation and not act accordingly?
- ☐ Always put off until tomorrow the efforts to improve my situation?
- ☐ Look for a shoulder to lean on or a helping hand so I can take the weight off?
- ☐ Find good excuses (even 1001) not to act?

☐ Missed out on because success is not happening?

☐ Talk to everyone about a problem without going directly to meet with the person(s) involved?

☐ Be constantly uncompromising toward me?

☐ Feel persecuted by others or by life itself?

☐ Identify my "executioner" and remain under their yoke?

☐ Constantly tell myself *I'm unlucky*?

☐ Make me sick just to be noticed, cuddled or better accepted?

☐ Sabotage beautiful projects or beautiful things in the process of being accomplished?

Summary Analysis

1. The more answers you check off, the more your behavior appears to be that of a victim.

2. As you review each one, try to answer this question in writing: "In what area of your life, or with whom, in particular, do you suffer from 'victimitis'?"

3. Write down the different items that you checked off and consider them as avenues to follow in order to reduce your rate of "victimitis."

Conclusions Regarding Your "Victimitis"

☐ If you checked off 4 answers or less: it's a positive balance (+).

☐ If you checked off 5 answers or more: it's a negative balance (-).

Record your result in your journal, in the table GPS / MY SELF-ESTEEM BALANCE SHEET, EXERCISE #9.

YOUR SENSE OF COMPETENCY

The real sense of competency allows you to be aware of your abilities, strengths and limitations in carrying out certain activities. It also includes the ability to take pride in your accomplishments and to be able to show them off. A healthy self-esteem is more focused on *being* rather than *showing*, which is linked to appearance, outcomes or performance.

Another dimension related to this sense is your willingness to solve problems effectively—that is, to be able to find the best possible solutions and to implement them.

Risks Related to a Weak Sense of Competency

For a large majority of people, their identity equates to their skills. In fact, their self-worth is intimately and absolutely linked to their achievements, so much so, that it even becomes easy for them to conclude afterwards that "I have no achievements, and thus, no value; in short, I am nothing!" No doubt, you have thought like that to yourself at least once in your life? It is certainly a common practice, yet it is very dangerous for self-esteem.

Besides, society is always there to reinforce this idea, hammering down that nail! Here is the proof: Just look what place we give or what consideration we show in regard to the disabled, people on welfare or the unemployed. They have no performance, therefore, no value nor even identity!

If your overall self-worth is very low, you may tend to invest in your sense of competency to compensate for "what you think of yourself"; in other words, you are going to strive *to do* more and more in order to hide this being that you are, that you devalue inside your mind.

This will become a "downward spiral" that traces the path to burnout. Essentially, if you do not recognize your true value within, you will tend to seek it externally, which will undoubtedly lead to imbalances in your self-esteem.

A weak sense of competency can also cause people not to take concrete action to solve their problems; they can procrastinate while wishing that the situation could be resolved by some miracle. Or better yet, they could offload their responsibilities onto the shoulders of those around them.

The great majority of people who are afraid of success or failure have a low sense of competency. I have met some very smart people who made themselves ill for fear of not being successful in life. Alain is an example of that.

Allan has not worked for over ten years. He was declared disabled, and lives off social assistance. He has a very high I.Q., but his intelligence has served to protect him to convince him that being mentally ill "is more socially acceptable" than having missed his shot in life. His fear of failure has been with him since he was a young boy, and it is in full control of him now. His fear of the responsibilities associated with success also paralyzes him. He can be qualified as a true perfectionist, in that he would rather stay put than make a mistake, no matter how small. Unfortunately, neither his numerous doctors nor I have yet been able to persuade him of his abilities.

EXERCICE # 10 GPS / COMPETENCY

Here are a few questions about your sense of competency. Answer by *yes* or *no*.

Points accorded for *yes*

1. Do I have difficulty expressing and promoting my professional skills?   -1

2. Do I frequently feel that I am not adequate?   -1

3. Am I afraid of success?   -1

4. Am I afraid of missing out on my shot at life?   -1

5. Do I ever waste great opportunities?   -1

6. Do I regularly fear being exposed and seen in my real light?   -1

7. Am I the type of person who, inside, hopes that someone would *finally* see my efforts?   -1

8. Do I recognize my parenting skills? My social skills?   2

9. Am I able to savor my successes?   2

10. When I encounter difficulties, do I give myself the means to resolve them?   2

For each *yes*, assign the corresponding points and add them up.   **TOTAL:** _____

Summary Analysis

1. The closer your score is to 6, the stronger your sense of competency seems.

2. If you have answered *yes* to question 1 and 5: your sense of competency is blocked from acting.

3. If you answered *yes* to questions 2, 6 and 7, your sense of competency is strongly linked to how others think of your performance.

4. Your self-talk tends to be hesitant or negative towards yourself if you answered *yes* to questions 3, 4 and 6. Your self-talk is constructive if you answered yes to questions 8 and 9.

5. Write down in your journal the items to which you answered *yes* for questions 1 to 7 inclusively, and *no* to the last three ones. They indicate what you have to work on to improve your feeling of competency.

Conclusions Regarding Your Sense of Competency

☐ If you have 4 points or more: it's a positive balance (+).

☐ If you have 3 points or less: it's a negative balance (-).

Record your result in your journal, in the table GPS / MY SELF-ESTEEM BALANCE SHEET, EXERCISE #10.

> *If I do not recognize myself internally for my true self-worth, I will seek it externally: which will lead to an unbalanced type of self-esteem*

The Types of Self-Esteem Related to Competency[16]

Here is a diagram depicting the various types of self-esteem obtained by combining two elements: *competency* and *self-worth*. It also lists the problems that can be caused by negative perceptions of *competency* and *self-worth*.

The arrangement of these two elements produces four possible combinations. The diagram therefore, presents four rectangles, which I will refer to as *quadrants*.

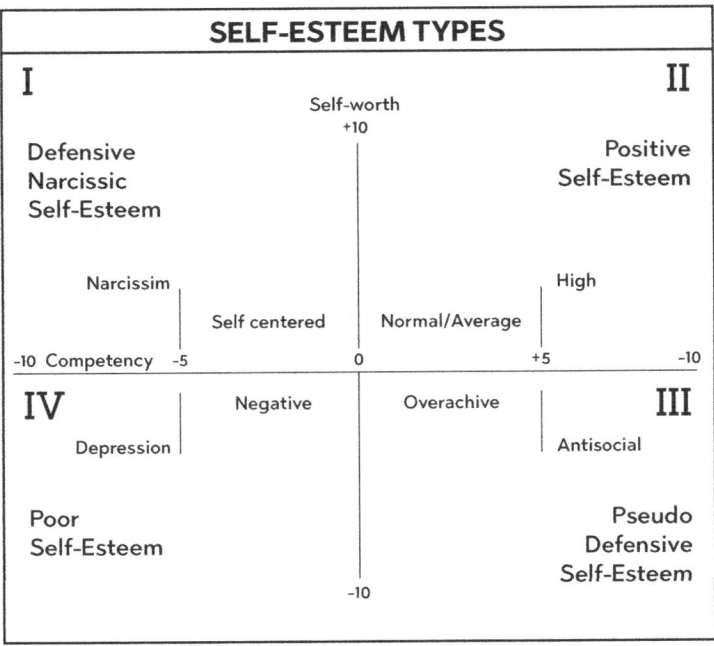

16 Mruk, Chris (1995). *Self-Esteem: Research, Theory and Practice*, p. 142

QUADRANT I: Defensive self-esteem, the narcissistic type;

QUADRANT II: Positive self-esteem;

QUADRANT III: Defensive self-esteem, the pseudo-type;

QUADRANT IV: Weak self-esteem.

For each of the types, I will explain them based on concrete examples.

Notes to the Reader

At the end of this section, you will have the opportunity to position yourself in one of the quadrants in order to determine the type of self-esteem that best represents you. In order to fully perceive the characteristics of the types represented, pay close attention to the descriptions that are given here.

Obviously, depending on what aspect of your life you are envisioning, you may position yourself with a different type of self-esteem. For example, you may perceive your job skills to be positive and your parenting skills to be "extremely competent." However, one type of self-esteem will usually predominate over others.

We develop different types of self-esteem to restore balance between unresolved wounds from our past and as a defense to avoid that suffering in the present. Most of the time, the initial injuries occurred in childhood, but became polarized in adulthood.

QUADRANT I: Defensive Self-Esteem, the Narcissistic Type (Competency -, Self-worth +), or the "I Can Do Everything" Syndrome

Here, we are dealing with a person who is more or less competent (competency -), but who has, in a way, developed their self-worth (self-worth +). They are the type of person who can seem very self-assured, overflowing with self-confidence, often ready to take on responsibilities that they cannot manage. In fact, the person believes they are better than they actually are.

This type of person is very self-centered, so much so that we say they are narcissistic[17], that is to say, very self-absorbed: they are the best, and often

---

17 In Greek mythology, Narcissus loved himself so much that he accidentally drowned himself in a lake while admiring the reflection of his face.

say it very openly to anyone who will hear it. In this category, we find the "know-it-all," the opportunists and the career oriented who seek to achieve their goals without necessarily having the required skills.

You can meet this kind of person in committees where they regularly offer to take on responsibilities which are often beyond their capacities. So the results are: they fail, or they do not meet the deadlines, but one thing is certain, they *always* have a good reason to justify themselves. They just do not see their limits, and this lack of awareness can only hurt them in the end.

Mary was a very competent person in her professional field. She was in a managerial position and was successful in that regard. Midway through her working life, she decided to make a career change and set up her own business. Note that she is also a beautiful woman who knows how to showcase herself and capitalize on her strengths to convince her clients that she is the ideal person for "almost anything." Without having experience in this new sector, she nevertheless convinced a client that she was able to resolve the situation in question. Thousands of dollars and many months later, since she was unable to deliver the goods, they mutually agreed to end their consulting contract.

QUADRANT II: Positive Self-Esteem (Competency +, Self-Worth +)

We define self-esteem as normal or healthy when a person has abilities (competency +5) for which they feel a positive sense of self-worth (self-worth +5). They know how to recognize their strengths and limitations, and are able to enjoy their successes and deal with failures in a reasonable way. This type of person, therefore, has a realistic perception of their abilities.

In this category, you will find people who are "comfortable in their own skin" and with whom it is pleasant to work. They take their place, they know how to take risks, all while recognizing their limits.

Further down the diagram, we also find people with higher self-esteem (competency +10, self-worth +10). They are aware of their self-esteem, and work to improve it and take good care of it. They also pay close attention to the self-esteem of others in their relationships.

At a conference, I had the opportunity to hear a professional speaker give a talk on self-esteem. This might sound fairly unremarkable until I mention that the speaker has multiple sclerosis (MS). **Wayne** is an outstanding communicator who, despite having some difficulty speaking, knows how to work a room, to make people laugh, and above all, make them reflect on the human condition. He impressed and moved many of the audience members. He was speaking to a room full of social workers, who were all in full possession of their means, physically and mentally, yet most of whom would not have had the necessary daringness to speak in front of such an audience. In my opinion, he epitomizes better than anyone the adage: "It's not the cards you're dealt, it's how you play them!"

QUADRANT III: Defensive Self-Esteem, Pseudo-Type (Competency +, Self-Worth -)

You will notice that many unbalanced self-esteem types develop in the area of positive competencies (competency +) associated with a negative self-worth (self-worth -). This undoubtedly reflects the emphasis placed, sometimes outrageously so, on performance in companies, as well as the negative consequences on the self-worth of workers. I associate the following syndromes with this type of self-esteem:

1. The "never good enough" syndrome;

2. The impostor syndrome;

3. The Cinderella syndrome.

The *pseudo* type has an image of themselves as fragile; their self-confidence is superficial. Repeat failures could, at times, even cause their self-esteem to collapse. They see themselves as less good than they really are.

1. The "Never Good Enough" Syndrome

This is a person who demonstrates competence (competency +), but who cannot recognize themselves as having them (self-worth -). Even if this person has real skills, their deficient sense of self-worth prevents them from being aware of their own abilities, as if they simply never acquired them.

This emptiness inevitably causes significant problems with stress related to their accomplishments; no matter what they succeed in, it is never enough for them to recognize their worth. Unable to taste their success, they take no satisfaction in doing so, and continually do more in order to prove their worth.

When we look at people with this type of self-esteem, we find "over-achievers," the perfectionists, the workaholics, and the overly devoted. On the extreme end of this combination (competency ++, self-worth -), we find an antisocial person whose life is based on the manipulation and exploitation of others, even if it means diminishing their value in order to increase their own. Having received little recognition from others, they give others a taste of their own medicine.

Many years ago, I began studying for a master's degree in business administration when I was a single parent, in a fairly precarious financial situation, with my mental state as poor as my finances. I studied for twelve months at full speed, of course, all without neglecting my family and financial responsibilities.

Despite succeeding with flying colors, I still couldn't savor my achievement. I reduced or even diminished its importance by making judgments about the quality of the degree, such as "It must not be worth that much, if I succeeded so easily..." A friend pointed out to me that I hadn't added MBA to my professional title; it is because I didn't dare to. I couldn't take any pride in it, and I didn't get any satisfaction from this respectable achievement.

It took me a few years, but I managed to internalize the value of my knowledge and acknowledge the effort I put into acquiring it. I finally added those three "big" official letters to my business card, and proudly displayed my diploma, which has become for me the symbol of my success. But above all, I reaped an added value: the pride in myself which I was finally able to recognize!

2. The Impostor Syndrome[18]

Doubts related to competency can cause some people to experience the impostor syndrome. These people tell themselves: "One day, people will realize that I am not as smart and efficient as they think I am." They feel as if they are cheaters and have a persistent fear of being found out. Among those who do not escape this duality are famous people / celebrities, many artists, politicians, etc.

3. The Cinderella Syndrome: Or When Humility Becomes Sin!

Others recognize certain abilities, but remain humble in the dark, hoping to finally be discovered and recognized. I call this attitude the Cinderella Syndrome to recall the fairytale in which the heroine was waiting to be discovered by Prince Charming. Here, the concept is seen in a broader light than in just romantic relationships, which, by the way, applies equally to women and men.

---

18 Rose-Clance, Pauline (1985). *The Impostor Phenomenon: Overcoming the Fear That Haunts Your Success.*

People with this type of self-esteem will, for example, be the type of employee who will work overtime without mentioning it, yet will keep an exact calculation of the hours worked. They secretly hope that their boss will notice it or take it into account during an employee evaluation. In this category, there are also people who hope to be considered for a promotion but who will not mention it, saying to themselves: "*One day, they will surely consider me, I put in so much effort*," and might we add, "*often in the shadows.*"

It is in this sense that humility becomes a sin: Cinderella does not give herself the right to assert her ambitions and aspirations: she is not entitled to them. Cinderella Syndrome is the precursor of the victim who—after many years of hoping to be recognized and unfortunately has not been—can become green, sick with depression or red with anger.

QUADRANT IV: Weak Self-Esteem (Competency—, Self-Worth -): Or the Syndrome of "I Am Nothing."

This type of person has a negative competency (competency -) with a negative perception of self-worth (self-worth -). They are the type of people who will describe themselves as "incapable," "without strengths," and who are convinced of their failure before even trying.

In this combination, you find the chronic negatives and the victims. Ultimately here, we also see the depressed person who is not capable of being competent, or even functional. They devalue themselves completely and can even go so far as to destroy themselves.

Pascal ended his life at the age of 25. He left a farewell letter to his parents, focusing on how he felt that he had ruined his life and that he had no hope of becoming anything.

EXERCISE # 11   **GPS / TYPES OF SELF-ESTEEM**

After reading the descriptions of the 4 types of self-esteem, locate yours in one of the quadrants in the previous diagram, according to your current perception.

Conclusions Regarding Your Type of Self-Esteem

☐ *If you position yourself in Quadrant II, your type of self-esteem is positive: write a (+) in the table.*

☐ *If you position yourself in Quadrant I, III, IV, your type of self-esteem is rather negative: write a (-) in the table.*

Record your result in your journal, in the table GPS / MY SELF-ESTEEM BALANCE SHEET, EXERCISE #11.

Compilation of the Table:
GPS / My Self-Esteem Balance Sheet

INSTRUCTIONS FOR THE GLOBAL COMPILATION
OF "GPS / BALANCE OF MY SELF-ESTEEM"

1. Return to your expedition journal in the table: GPS / Balance Sheet.

2. Calculate the *total* number of + and – in each corresponding column.

3. Take note of the *date* on which you make the first assessment. You can review it another time to compare your progress.

4. Read the CONCLUSION items that apply to you.

5. If convenient, apply the suggestions you will find at the end of this chapter in "What To Do Next?" to improve your self-esteem.

Table: GPS / My Self-Esteem Balance Sheet

You have permission to reproduce this table in your expedition journal, for personal use only. By completing this table from the exercises suggested above, you will be able to get the GPS of your self-esteem at this point in your life.

Please note:

This assessment can be obtained either by following the systematic method, through exercises OR following the spontaneous method. However, it will give you a better indicator if you use the first method. For more information, refer to the Notes to the Readers at the beginning of chapter 3.

Number	Exercices	+	-
1	The Strength of My Self-Esteem - Faced with success - Faced with a compliment - Faced with failure - Faced with a criticism		
2	My Self-Esteem Thermometer		
3	My Self-Esteem per Life Sphere - Family - Financial - Physical - Romantic Relationships - Social - Professional / Work		
4	My Sense of Identity (GPS / Identity)		
5	My Dignity (GPS / Dignity)		
6	My Sense of Security (GPS / Security)		
7	My Sense of Belonging (GPS / Belonging)		
8	My Sense of Determination (GPS / Determination)		
9	My "Victimitis" (GPS / "Victimitis")		
10	My Sense of Competency (GPS / Competency)		
11	Type of Self-Esteem Related to My Competency and My Self-Worth (GPS / Types of Self-Esteem)		
TOTAL	GPS / MY SELF-ESTEEM BALANCE SHEET Date:		

CONCLUSIONS: GPS / MY SELF-ESTEEM BALANCE SHEET

To analyze your balance sheet as an accountant would, you need to assess the following two elements:

1. The last line or the *total obtained*. This final result is a global indicator. It is very interesting in itself because it shows you, at a glance, which side your self-worth leans.

2. Each line or *all the components* that constitute your overall self-esteem. It is by scrutinizing each one that you will become aware of the item(s) on which you need to invest time and energy in order to improve it, or bring it to a level that you find satisfactory.

The Total Obtained

Consider this compilation as a profile of your self-esteem. Do you recognize yourself? Depending on the results, you will get by adding up the total in the line "GPS / MY SELF-ESTEEM BALANCE SHEET", there are *roughly* these three possibilities.

THE BALANCE SHEET IS POSITIVE. The number of (+) obtained greatly exceeds the number of (-). It means that you demonstrate good self-esteem. Stay alert and vigilant in keeping your self-esteem as balanced as possible.

However, you may still have noticed some improvements that can be made to any of the components that you assigned a negative (-) value to. Try to console yourself; No one is perfect!

THE BALANCE SHEET IS NEUTRAL. You obtain an equivalent, or almost, number of (+) and (-); It can happen. The important thing here will be to further analyze each of the components assessed and instead focus on the actions that can be taken to positively develop your level of self-esteem.

THE BALANCE SHEET IS NEGATIVE. Your balance sheet shows a negative balance, do you have more (-) than (+)? This is not very encouraging; you realize that there is much more to improve compared to what you are satisfied with. Do not despair; You are already on the right track as you are now more conscious of where you are. This is already your first step in the right direction to improving your self-esteem.

Please Note

Your balance sheet can indicate whether you are living *your* life, or rather a life recommended by others. Indeed, a positive self-esteem is a good indication that you are going in the right direction, on your path to your life's mission. On the other hand, significant issues related to types of low self-esteem indicate that you are on the wrong path. What is your impression: are you on *your* path? At your X? Are you satisfied with what you are experiencing? Are you fulfilled?

GOOD NEWS FOR ALL! All hopes are allowed. Self-esteem is not static and can always be improved; there is no age for that. It is up to you to go further on this little-traveled path of personal development and learn to use the right tools, or how to apply them if you already know what they are.

Analysis of the Balance Sheet Components

To further your assessment, you can review the definitions of the various senses that interest you. Once the excitement of the exercises has passed, you may want to take a break to take stock of the situation.

THE POSITIVE ELEMENTS. Take time to write down which of the elements you are satisfied with. Are there many? Which ones are surprising to you? Which sense are you most proud of? After having put so much effort into performing these exercises in order to define your self-esteem profile, you deserve to take a break for a few minutes to savor the results!

Keep this table handy; it can be used to remind you of your strengths during periods when you may be more inclined to diminish their value.

THE ELEMENTS "TO BE DEVELOPED." This is a crucial moment for you; you now know which sense you must invest energy into in order to raise your self-esteem. It is certainly more interesting than simply having a vague idea that makes it hard to know what to do or where to start. Do you have several?

Which ones surprise you? Which sense did you wish to improve in the first place?

Analysis According to Two Axes

I have mentioned before, in the definitions section, that self-esteem can be seen as having two axes: what touches your *being*, and how you *act*. Here is how I divided the various senses between these two axes:

1. Self-esteem affecting your being (respect, dignity, love, self-worth):

   - A Sense of identity;
   - Dignity;
   - "Victimitis";
   - A Sense of belonging.

2. Self-esteem affecting your actions (confidence, self-affirmation, abilities, choices, learning):

    - A Sense of Security;

    - A Sense of Belonging;

    - A Sense of Determination;

    - A Sense of Competency.

The strength of your self-esteem and the self-esteem thermometer have not been included here because they include too many points that could be classified in either of these two categories. As for the sense of belonging, it seems plausible to include it on both axes.

I encourage you to verify in which axes your strengths lie? And which sense(s) "to be developed"? Write them down, this will help you make the most relevant choice among the tools that I will present to you below.

What To Do Next?

1. Discover Why You Most Want to Better Your Self-Esteem

Keep in mind that it may be easier to work on the *action* axis because the results may appear faster and seem more tangible. In many cases, it will also take energy to discover the wonderful being that you are. And trust me, while it may take longer, it is well worth it.

Depending on the results you have obtained and the analysis you have made at this point, *a decision remains to be made* whether or not to continue with this process. To be able to make this choice, you should find out *why* you think you need to value yourself more?

How important is this to you? Is it a question of pleasure in general? To be happier? For your mental health? Or is it more a matter of life and death?

After reflecting on these questions, you will surely find the means to answer them. It seems that when the student is ready, the teacher appears.

2. How to Take Care of Your Self-Esteem

In the first few chapters of this *book*, several pieces of practical information were offered to you. The next few chapters will be devoted to techniques and tools to help you maintain or regenerate your self-esteem. Dive in!

If it does not end up being enough for you and you prefer to go further, there are *workshops* out there on this topic. They can be of help to you as needed.

Also, do not hesitate to consult with someone if you feel as if you are going in circles. There are specialists out there that will be able to accompany you on *this great adventure of loving yourself more.*

CHAPTER 4

SURVIVAL KIT: OR HOW TO MAINTAIN YOUR SELF-ESTEEM FLOWER

*Far from being hostile...
the forest was generous with those who knew
the secrets of its flora and fauna.*[19]

19 Descheneaux, Jean-Georges (1990). *Guide pratique de survie en forêt Canadienne. (A Practical Survival Guide in Canadian Forests)*, p.8.

Survival Kit

Survival Techniques Through Self-Esteem

If it is to survive, every flower needs special care. The same principles apply to our self-esteem; appropriate care must be given on a regular basis; otherwise it may wither away.

In this section, I suggest techniques to preserve, as well as possible, each sense related to your self-esteem, or to improve it if necessary. These techniques come with concrete tools and exercises so that you can easily practice them to "re-energize" your self-esteem flower. One section is specifically dedicated to the work sector.

In addition, there will also be an overview of what fosters self-esteem in children and teenagers. I also reserve a few thoughts for the elderly.

Basic Equipment

Are you well equipped to face life and fully experience this expedition that will last many years – in other words, your entire life?

Any expedition requires basic equipment, also known as a survival kit, which includes multiple items essential to get someone through the *normal* conditions associated with the kind of trek planned. For example, a survival kit for a forest exploration would include, among other things: matches, toilet paper, a compass, a hatchet, a few utensils, a flashlight, bandages, medical tape, etc.

For a boat trip, you would probably add life jackets, life preservers, fishing rods, etc. Surprisingly, for any type of expedition, it is always recommended to include a pad of paper and a pencil.

For our purposes, we will consider self-esteem as the basic element of survival. What is somewhat paradoxical here is that self-esteem is both the goal (we want to improve it) and the tool, to help you discover your personal power and guarantee your passport to health.

"COACH'S" TIP: YOUR EXPEDITION JOURNAL!

So far, you must have found it to be VERY beneficial to have a journal for all the exercises you have chosen to do. This journal will become precious to you!

What Can You do to Maintain Your Self-Esteem?

Here is a summary of the basic techniques, related to each of the Five Senses, which are essential for your self-esteem to survive. We will elaborate on them later in this section:

✔ **Giving myself the right to dream and knowing where I am going;**

✔ **Knowing myself and increasing my self-worth;**

✔ **Accepting myself and learning to receive;**

✔ **Having a network and asserting myself;**

✔ **Knowing my abilities and recognizing myself.**

You have certainly heard these suggestions before, and I can assure you that they will have absolutely no effect on you *unless* you put them into practice. These techniques are not magic, if you simply read them without applying them, they will not work. Sorry to disappoint you!

So why not make the decision now to take the necessary steps and move forward in the direction of your choice? Every little improvement that you make for yourself will necessarily affect your overall sense of self-worth.

When to Maintain it?

Around ten years ago, the advertising for my self-esteem workshops read as follows: "*As with physical exercise, the habit of helping yourself is also a question of daily training.*"

> *For each improvement brought to one of the Five Senses of self-esteem, there will also be an increase in your sense of overall self-worth.*

I remain convinced that it is vital to take care of our self-esteem flower on a **daily** basis. Develop the reflex, the instinct, to take a few minutes every day *just for you*: to please yourself, or at least, to recognize your accomplishments. Putting everyone and everything ahead of ourselves is how our self-esteem deteriorates.

Self-esteem is our mental health, so we are talking about basic hygiene, just psychological rather than physical. You take a bath or shower every day; how about giving yourself a minimum daily ritual of five to ten minutes just for yourself? The idea is to improve your psychological "tone." What if this were covered by your health insurance, would you be willing to invest a little more time in it?

Do you know about the torture technique where the little drops of water hitting you over time slowly drive you mad? Or how the strength of water droplets will sculpt a rock over time? The same goes for self-esteem: little by little, it shapes your life.

Just remember that every improvement made, or care given to any of the Five Senses of self-esteem will fully invigorate that flower, and at the same time, will enhance your overall self-worth.

Practical Techniques and Tools

Here you will find a series of complementary techniques and tools that will be used to improve each of the senses underlying self-esteem. I chose to start with the sense of determination because, as previously mentioned, it is a necessary prerequisite to undertake any developmental process. It is the *reason* that pushes us to act, to find out *how* to do it.

IMPROVING MY SENSE OF DETERMINATION

✔ **TECHNIQUES:** Giving myself the right to dream
Knowing where I am going

🛟 **Tools:** My map or the lists of my aspirations
Three precious lists

✔ GIVING MYSELF THE RIGHT TO DREAM

The book *The Dolphin: Story of a Dreamer* is a wonderful tale that makes us understand that within each of us lies a source that is filled with buried treasure: our dreams. The dolphin is told: "There are some things that cannot be seen with your eyes. You must see them with your heart, and that is the hardest part. If you can rediscover within yourself the spirit of the little dolphin that you once were, with all your memories and dreams, you will make your way together through this adventure called life, always trying to cope with existence as best you can. And your heart will never become overwhelmed or grow old…"[20]

---

20 Bambaren, Sergio (1995). *The Dolphin: Story of a Dreamer.*

✔ KNOWING WHERE I AM GOING

☉ My map or my lists of aspirations

In the previous sections, you located your level of self-esteem and now the next step is to clarify where you want to go: *What are my life goals?* I mentioned before that your road map for the expedition of your life translates into your list of goals. The ultimate destination being the fulfillment of your life's mission, which is to be true to yourself, to your true self.

A question of priorities: Do you spend more time preparing your grocery list or your annual vacation compared to the trip of your life? What are your goals? Your values? Your aspirations? Your mission?

There are several books that can help you in building your list. Without necessarily going into details on the techniques for setting goals, it is vital to have a list, even just an outline, of your life's goals; to know what you want to be, what you want to do and have. Keep this list handy so that you can review it periodically.

In my workshops, I explain the phenomenal principle by which written goals are achieved almost 97% of the time, while the average drops to around 70% for goals that were *only thought about in our head.*

We can then imagine what can happen if we do not have a specific plan, not even in our head... This idea is reflected in *Alice in Wonderland.* Alice asks the March Hare which path she should take, and he responds by asking Alice where she wants to go. Alice replies that she does not know, so the March Hare retorts, "If you don't know where you are going, how will you know when you have arrived?"

If you do not already know of any techniques for discovering or setting goals, you might find it useful to learn about some. For our purposes, we will stick to three practical and very simple lists that will guide you in establishing the direction you want your life to take. It is never too late to add success to your life, if you choose it *now.*

☉ Three Precious Lists

(1) What I want to eliminate from my life; (2) What I want in my life; (3) What I am grateful for in my life.

1. What I Want to Eliminate From My Life

When you want to take stock of where you are in your life's journey, you may often neglect to clarify *what you no longer want*; which is essential! For, in addition to naming what you no longer want in your life, it allows you to clarify your limits as to what is no longer acceptable. This is an endpoint that you want to make, and this list supports your decision. This is a good opportunity to develop your assertiveness.

2. What I Want in My Life

Having goals or projects is the spice of life! It gives you energy and helps you stay the course during life's storms. This is true for all ages: in childhood, to learn to settle down and carry out projects; for youth, often lost in the face of the multitude of choices to make; in adulthood, so as not to become disillusioned by routine; and for retirees and seniors, so as not to be bored or discouraged, waiting for life to end, without enjoying it.

In his book *Success Is Not an Accident*[21], *Tommy Newberry* tells the true story of John Goddard who, at the young age of fifteen, wrote an extensive list of 127 goals he dreamed of for his future. It ranged from exploring the great rivers of the world, to climbing Mount Everest and Vesuvius, to going to medical school, learning photography, piloting, and so much more. Although he dropped a few of them along the way, by the age of forty-seven, he had about twenty goals left to complete, several of which were already in progress.

Inspiring, isn't it? The moral of this story is that a carefully written list makes for the adventure that managing your life can afford! This holds true for everyone.

This should not be too hard for you; you just have to let your wishes come forth, the interests that you often talk about, or the ones you have buried under the carpet for so long. Do not censor yourself, there will always be time to do that later.

Keep this list alive; take care of it! Check back regularly and keep a record of your accomplishments. This is great for improving your sense of determination and competency.

3. What I am Grateful for in My life

This list, which may seem quite unusual for most people, allows you to appreciate what you currently benefit, but often take for granted. By developing and revising it regularly, it strengthens your ability to enjoy your possessions and helps you feel like less of an unlucky or helpless victim.

I met someone who suffers from sleep apnea. This illness forces him to wear a specialized mask every night that provides him with the oxygen he needs to survive; otherwise, he could die of suffocation. Since that time, I have thanked life for the natural function of breathing freely, which usually goes unnoticed,

---

21 Newberry, Tommy (1999). *Success is Not an Accident.*

especially since I do not have any form of breathing problems. It is so easy to take our health, and our bodies for granted.

I believe that life, as a friend, appreciates being warmly recognized, and in turn, gives back to us generously. Learn to consider life as an ally; it is good to say why you love and appreciate it; it will be able to give back to you in abundance.

What Happens Next!

These three lists must remain alive; do not hide them at the back of a drawer as soon as you finish writing them down. Keep them close to you, in a diary for example, where you can consult them regularly and enrich the third list with your life's blessings. You might also want to refer to it at times when you will have more difficulty appreciating what is going on.

For the past twenty years, **Lilian**, a friend, has kept all the photos or images of the goals she has achieved. And believe me, there are many, because she is a great dreamer and builder. She confided in me that this treasure chest was a good morale boost at times when she was going through an existential crisis in relation to her sense of identity. Note to interested parties!

You are the Captain of Your Expedition

You now have the two essential tools that you will need in hand for any expedition.

1. Your **road map** now that you have listed your goals, this road map specifies **where** you want to go;

2. And your **self-esteem** from the GPS balance sheet, your compass that points your way.

As you are the captain of this expedition of a lifetime, I can guide you as to the most favorable conditions to reach your destination, but the rest is up to you.

Keep in mind that you have power over your destiny; *nothing is predetermined!* But, in order to do this, you have to realize that *no one but yourself has* the ability to make you happy; only you have the ability to get you to *your* chosen destination. It is only you who can make the decision to improve yourself and your living conditions by removing the barriers you have erected thus far.

A long time ago, I read a story that really struck me. A man had been convicted and put in a dungeon; he served his sentence for over 20 years. One day, when he could no longer bear the suffering of his imprisonment, he decided to escape. He pushed on the door to his cell and realized it was not locked… In fact, it had never been! How many times have we remained locked in by our own limits? What are your limits?

Linda does not like her neighborhood, and she has had enough of her house. To be honest, she has secretly dreamed of having a country house off-and-on now for 20 years. Yet she still has not moved.

> *Each of us guards a gate of change that can only be opened from the inside.*
> **The Aquarian Conspiracy**

Who is forcing her to stay? What is preventing her from changing houses? Neighborhoods? Towns?

Why does she agree to suffer her fate without acting? The answer lies within her and most certainly comes from her own history, her past and from her beliefs. It is clear that she is just putting up with her life and that she will continue to do so until the day she realizes that she is the captain of her own ship, the writer and director of HER own life.

IMPROVING MY SENSE OF IDENTITY

✔ TECHNIQUES: Knowing myself
Increasing my self-worth

⊕ Tools: Listening to my inner voice
List of my characteristics
My life's mission
Affirming: "I am unique"

✔ KNOWING MYSELF

⊕ Listening to my Inner Voice

Your inner voice reveals to you your likes and dislikes, your values, your beliefs, your aspirations, everything that you are truly about. Unfortunately, circumstances are such that you often forget this voice, or force it to be silent; many do not even know that it exists anymore.

Being in touch with your inner voice means rooting yourself in the authenticity of your feelings, instead of wanting to possess a quality that is not truly yours just to please those around you.

Often, people with low self-esteem have a tendency to no longer feel their emotions; they lose touch with their own feelings. It can even go so far as the individual no longer being able to feel their hunger, desires, tastes or displeasure. This would partly explain their inability to say no.

How can you manage to no longer be in touch with yourself? In short, I would say that your upbringing probably contributed to it, but even more so, your personal reaction to your environment, where you wanted to do everything to please others and be loved to the point of almost no longer existing.

Here is a simple exercise that can help you to reconnect with yourself.

Exercise: My Feelings

When we talk about *feeling*, it is to have sensations, physical perceptions and emotions. These impressions can be *very* light, so if you are not absolutely careful, you may not even feel them. If you are the type of person who is constantly moving around, unable to stop, it is normal for you not to hear that small inner voice; you will probably have to do a lot of practicing before you are able to perceive it.

But the important thing for you is knowing that you have this voice within you. The goal of this exercise is for you to learn how to detect the signs that this voice uses to speak to you. So how do you do it?

For a few days, you will practice questioning your "feelings" before responding to anything, like what you want to eat, for an outing that is offered to you, a destination to choose from, really for anything involving a choice.

Preparing Yourself

You may prefer to do a warm-up, just to prepare yourself. At rest, try to clear your mind for a few minutes by cutting off your flow of thoughts. Look at what is going on inside you: at the level of the heart, or the solar plexus[22]: What do you smell? What do you feel? Take a few moments to be in touch with yourself.

This can sound strange to a more rational person, but it is easy to do and the results are amazing: Give it a try.

The Exercise

Here is how to do it. *When you have a decision or a choice to make*:

1. Ask yourself the question to which you want to find a solution;
2. Try to feel the energy passing through the solar plexus or your heart;

---

22 Solar plexus: center of the sympathetic nervous system situated in the abdomen between the stomach and the spinal column.

3. Rate the energy or sensation that you feel, from 1 to 5.

For example:

Give a rating of 1 if your feeling is unpleasant, nonexistent or if your energy declines. For some people, it makes them want to say something like "yuck!" as a spontaneous rejection. These kinds of reactions tell you that you either do not want whatever it is, or that you are not interested in it.

Give the rating of 5 if your sensation is pleasant and present, or if your energy increases. For some, it makes them say something like "wow!" as an exclamation of enthusiasm. These types of reactions tell you that you want it, or that you are interested in it.

4. Respect what your "inner voice" is telling you by your energy level! So, if it is pleasant, do it, put your idea into practice; otherwise, abstain!

If you are unfamiliar with this kind of exercise and want to develop a connection with your intuition, then feel free to practice it over and over. With time, the answer will come to you almost instantly, with clarity, and you will learn to trust your little inner voice.

✔ INCREASING MY SELF-WORTH

◎ Making the List of my Characteristics

If I asked you point-blank to mention three of your best qualities and three of your shortcomings, would you be able to respond quickly? Or would it take a long time to think about it?

If I increase the difficulty level of the question by telling you that you cannot include the two qualifiers "honest and hard-working" (I take it for granted that you are both of these things), what about now? Are you at a loss? And if I now ask you for 50? Or 60? What will your reactions be? Impossible, you would say; I have never had that many qualities!

Think again! And to prove it to you, I invite you to do the following exercise, which will surely convince you. I suggest you do it on two levels: the rational level and at the internalization level.

Two Levels of Exercise

1. The Rational Level

As part of my self-esteem workshops, I made up a list of all possible adjectives that can be found in the dictionary, and the participants only have to check off the ones they thought applied to them, regardless to which degree (a little or a lot). Some had counted as many as 200, yet had initially had trouble mentioning just 2 spontaneously.

You can perform this exercise now by listing out all of the adjectives that apply to you from the dictionary, from A to Z. For the sake of space, I will list only a few here as examples.

Affable – Affectionate – Benevolent – Caring – Combative – Conciliatory – Disciplined – Discreet – Elegant – Energetic – Fair – Faithful – Genuine – Honest – Impatient – Intelligent – Jovial –Lucky – Mature – Natural – Opportunist – Patient – Passionate – Positive – Punctual – Quick – Rational – Reasonable – Reserved – Resolute – Responsible – Sensual – Simple – Skillful – Sociable – Tender – Thorough – Unique – Vigilant – Vigorous – Wise.

Of course, you can continue the exercise by adding all of the qualifiers that describe who you are, and all that you can do.

I suggest that you regularly review your characteristics, *learn them by heart,* and be able to talk about them easily and be comfortable assigning them to yourself.

As for your faults, which are often easier to list out, I like to say that they are just "qualities waiting to be developed." Consider them as such in the future, or as challenges for you to overcome. This will make you focus more on taking action to improve them, versus focusing on what is wrong.

2. The Internalizing Level

To internalize the belief in your qualities, this visualization exercise can be very useful.

The point here is to use your imagination and make EACH of your qualities penetrate deep inside yourself.

Exercise: Internalizing Your Qualities

Relax and take several deep breaths. Clear your mind, and proceed as follows:

1. Choose a quality you wish to internalize or integrate deep within yourself (ex., simplicity).

2. Imagine that this quality is a friend that you love very much, and she is coming to visit you. Welcome her warmly, take her tenderly in your arms and let this warmth flow through and permeate your being. The essence of simplicity is now entering you.

3. Taste it. Congratulate yourself! You now have simplicity!

4. Do not hesitate to say that you possess this quality, even if you still wish to improve it even more.

Repeat this exercise for any other characteristic that you wish to internalize or integrate into yourself.

Exercise: Forgiving Yourself

You can redo this internalization exercise at any time to help you forgive yourself for your flaws or, as we said earlier, your "qualities waiting to be developed." You are not perfect and you probably never will be; for your personal balance, you must learn to accept and forgive yourself for your mistakes, shortcomings and emotions. To love them.

As soon as you tenderly welcome a part of yourself that you do not appreciate (your jealousy, your impatience, etc.), you will be surprised to see that it will slowly fade away. One thing is for sure, it will be much easier for you to work on improving it after doing this exercise of acceptance.

◎ My Life's Mission

More and more, we hear the term "mission in life" mentioned. There is a strong link between knowing our mission and our self-esteem: "When a person understands their reason for being on this planet and then lives being motivated by their ultimate goal, their level of esteem is always remarkable[23]."

We are free to choose our mission, it is not predetermined: it is up to us to decipher it by probing the depths of our soul. Our mission is definitely linked to our interests and our passion, but not necessarily to our work.

It is never too late to discover and achieve your mission. In his book *Illusions: The Adventures of a Reluctant Messiah*, Richard Bach says: "If you are not dead, your mission is not finished." In Jean Monbourquette's book[24], which I highly recommend, he specifies that there are two ideal periods in life when the "call to our mission" is particularly felt, first in adolescence and then in middle age.

Do not hesitate to take this step in discovering your mission if you do not already know it; its discovery will give meaning to your existence. First, you will have to complete your "inner housekeeping" to be able to reach your destination, because it is almost impossible to carry out your mission if you are overwhelmed by the deep wounds of your past. Although, this does not prevent you from trying to identify what your mission in life is.

---

23 Lebon, Violette (1999). *L'essentiel: l'estime de soi (The Essential: Self-Esteem)*, p.16

24 Monbourquette, Jean (2001). *À chacun sa mission, découvrir son projet de vie (To Each His Own Mission. Discovering Your Life Project)*.

Exercise: If I Only Had Six Months to Live

Open your expedition journal.

Take this exercise as seriously as possible. For a few minutes, imagine what would really mean the most to you if you only had a few months to live. Let us suppose you are healthy during this period. Listen to your heart. Take the time you need to let the *real things* come to the surface.

If I only had six months to live _____

_____

_____

_____

_____

_____

_____

In my case, I did this exercise nearly 30 years ago and I remember it as if it were yesterday. While writing it, I was in tears, I felt it as vividly as if I really had only six months to live. It took me at least 10 years to achieve what I had discovered, all because my self-esteem wouldn't let me go in that direction; at the time, my ego was firmly at the helm. It wasn't until I healed some of my wounds that I was finally able to get on the road to my destination.

In many cases, the answers found in this exercise reveal elements of your personal mission. After having done the exercise, you might want to ask yourself some more questions to gauge how far you are from your mission.

1. Am I being the person I want to be and doing what I would like to do if I were going to die?

2. What is preventing me from starting now?

3. How can I integrate an action or activity in my daily life that leads in the direction of my mission?

🛟 Affirming: "I am Unique"

By recognizing your achievements and your mission and by reclaiming your specific qualities, you will come to see your uniqueness. You will become more and more convinced that there is no one else who has your exact mix of qualities, flaws, experiences and acquired knowledge. You are unique in this world! Savor this belief and why not convince yourself of it in writing by completing this statement:

I am unique because _____

_____

_____

_____

_____

_____

IMPROVING MY SENSE OF SECURITY

✔ **TECHNIQUES:** Accepting myself
Choosing myself as a priority
Learning to receive
Soothing my moods

🛟 **Tools:** The mirror
Centering myself
The 10% risk games

✔ ACCEPTING MYSELF

🛟 The Mirror

We cannot change what we despise. We must first make peace with this enemy to be able to then transform it. This same principle applies to us. If we hate a part of our body or our personality, we will always experience internal confrontations without the possibility of change.

The goal of this exercise is for you to unconditionally accept your physique. It might sound silly or even stupid to you, but it has been proven to work in many participants, particularly with women, as they have used this exercise much more frequently than the male participants. It is a first step in the direction of achieving a better self-image.

The Mirror Exercise

Even if you are feeling very resistant to this exercise, for the next few days in a row, practice it morning and night, ideally for two weeks.

Stand completely naked in front of a mirror, observe yourself and pay attention to what you are feeling: the discomfort, the uneasiness. Then, for a minute or two, repeat, "I totally accept myself, without the slightest reservation."

Focus on your reflection. Breathe deeply. Give yourself time to get those words out. You will be surprised at how powerful this exercise is, especially if you have any complaints about how your body looks.

✔ CHOOSING MYSELF AS A PRIORITY

In the turmoil of our professional and family activities, the heavy weight of the accumulated roles we have to respect can make us lose sight of our own existence. This is especially true for women who are the heads of families, workaholics and perfectionists. I have seen more than one person suffer from frequent ailments: insomnia, migraines, etc. They did not have a single minute to themselves, which created a downward spiral for their health, both physically and mentally.

At one time, I was overcome with stress. The circumstances led me to start getting my nails done by a manicurist. In terms of my budget, getting my nails done was madness. In terms of my psychological survival, it was THE necessary vital breath of air to keep me from suffocating under the pressure. To be in touch with myself in the moment.

I held on to life ... thanks to my nails: Pathetic, isn't it? But in my case, it really was beneficial.

Making yourself a priority means that certain principles will have to be let go, for example, the idea of being perfect or that EVERYTHING you do must be perfect. In your case, what is keeping you from "losing it"? What keeps you centered? Is it gardening? Tinkering? Cooking? Walking in nature? Meditating? Doing sports? Taking a few days away from everything and everyone?

And especially, when do you do it? How often do you allow yourself to prioritize? Do you wait until you are at your wit's end? I knew a young mother who would advance her wake up time just to make sure she got to enjoy some free time before the morning rush. This was *her* time to prioritize herself.

✔ LEARNING TO RECEIVE

Sometimes great things happen in our lives that we do not accept right away, especially if our life thus far has been tumultuous, filled with storms or hurricanes. When the good weather sets in, it can be hard to believe that nature will continue to be kind.

Whether it is the emotional security or the financial security that you want to see restored in your life, you need to start believing that you can really attain it. It may sound strange to you, but a lot of people are afraid of success. You have to make space within yourself to receive what you are yearning or aspiring for; otherwise, you will find a way to sabotage the beautiful, positive things that come your way.

After my divorce, I lived as a single mother for a few years, the time to heal my wounds, follow my compass, and retrace my map. Then, I met my spouse who I am still with right now. For our first anniversary together, we celebrated at our favorite places, and we talked about our relationship, which we considered to be wonderful, complete, and very fulfilling for each of us.

However, I was experiencing a strange feeling, one that I was having a hard time identifying, but which I defined as follows. This wonderful year filled with sweetness and harmony is like a gift whose delights I savor every day ... but can that be loved? That simple, that easy? I called it my quiet happiness. Deep down, I didn't believe it could last... And by sharing this with him, he who had taught me to receive, I dared to show my vulnerability, I took one more step in his direction, and it made me feel more secure emotionally.

✔ SOOTHING MY MOODS

Here are two additional tools that will allow you, along with the first one, to restore calm, and to gently push your limits by applying the second.

⊕ Centering Myself

Use this exercise when you are tired, depressed, anxious or sad... I recommend doing the exercise as often as possible; at first, do this many times a day if need arises. The more you put it into practice, the more the feeling of well-being will set in, so you won't need to be as systematic about the exercise afterwards.

The goal is to be able to center your three bodies (physical, emotional and energetic), through thought or mental imagery, so as to be:

1. More balanced and serene;

2. In touch with your inner source;

3. Closer to your intuitions;

4. More open to solving a challenge;

5. More creative in finding new ideas.

Exercise: Centering

- *Know to recognize when you are not centered, means off-center.* Examples: distressed, confused, sad, upside down or, "out of sorts."

- *AND also be aware of when you have enough control to bring your mind back to "the center" of yourself.*

A. Close your eyes;

B. Imagine your three bodies as three concentric circles that overlap with each other to form only one circle;

C. Repeat to yourself: "*I am in touch and centered*";

D. Associate a specific gesture with the exercise (e.g.: joining the tip of your index with the tip of your thumb);

E. Then, let a creative thought rise from your inner SOURCE deep in the center of these three circles, and feel it, as if it is floating through your subconscious and finally making itself known to your conscious mind.

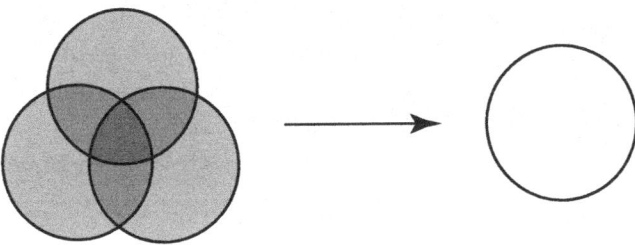

- Once you are used to it, this exercise can be done without having to close your eyes.

🎲 The 10% Risk Games

Many people feel anxious about a new project or activity if they have never done anything like it before. It is often difficult to coolly change our habits because of the possible risk of failure; that is why I am suggesting this "10% Risk Games."

Do not go all in, only gamble for 10% more risk. Add or accept 10% more discomfort in an area that makes you feel insecure, and take action.

Here are some examples that complete this sentence: "If I accepted 10% discomfort …:

- *In my work...* ←→ I would look for a position that I like rather than accepting one solely on the basis of ideal conditions;

- *In my career...* ←→ I would qualify for the promotion I am offered;

- *In my romantic relationship...* ←→ I would agree to show my vulnerability more;

- *In my finances...* ←→ I would adopt a budget;

- *In my contact with clients...* ←→ I would dare to use a new method.

In your case, what would be the extra step that you would take for only 10% risk?

IMPROVING MY SENSE OF BELONGING

✔ **TECHNIQUES:** Having a network
Building a quality network
Asserting myself

◎ **Tools:** Forming a support group
Knowing how to appreciate
and express it
Knowing when to say yes or no

✔ HAVING A NETWORK

Each of us needs to feel connected to someone or something: Abraham Maslow included this in his hierarchy of human needs. Social self-esteem develops when we realize how important we are to our peers. We then "feel involved in a relational network, a social niche with which we identify. The feeling of belonging then becomes the antidote to feelings of social isolation.[25]"

Moreover, very serious studies have shown the impact of family or social support on people's physical health, whether it is related to heart disease or certain cancers; you will find an excellent overview in Guy Corneau's book, La guérison du cœur[26].

Hence the evidence for the importance of building a network, however small, for a balanced emotional life and a balanced psyche. It is a choice to make. It is a decision that needs to be made.

✔ BUILDING A QUALITY NETWORK

Whether it is a question of obtaining information, knowledge or support, everyone creates a network of relationships, even informal ones, and has always done so. In fact, we see more and more groups forming to overcome increasing social isolation in both the professional and personal domains.

A network of relationships is crucial to your career, we will get to that later, but for now we will focus more on the meaning of your social network and the impact it has on your self-esteem.

---

25 Reasoner, Robert, (1988). *Building Self-Esteem.*
26 Guy Corneau (2000), *La Guérison du cœur (The Healing of the Heart).*

Here is a proposed ACTION PLAN to build your network:

1. Specify the goals you are pursuing in order to maintain the relationships you currently have or to develop new ones. What do you no longer want in terms of relationship style? What exactly are you looking for?

   POSSIBLE ANSWERS: *to have fun, play a sport with people who have the same values, have in-depth exchanges...*

2. Go over each person or group you have come into contact with and assess the effect this relationship has on your self-esteem. To make this exercise easier, you can give yourself a rating of 1 to 5 where

   - A rating of 1 corresponds to: "I feel tired or unmotivated after each meeting";

   - A rating of 3: "Most of the time, I feel good after we meet"; or

   - A rating of 5 which is equivalent to: "After each meeting, my energy is better."

   To concretely illustrate this idea, here is an example:

   Nicole says: "When I play tennis with Paul, he has the gift of making me feel like a beginner with every stroke; he is of a much higher caliber than me, but after two years I think I have improved. I have the impression that in order to keep the upper hand, he prefers not to see my good shots. It annoys me royally and I no longer enjoy playing with him. (She gave a rating 1.)

   On the other hand, the times she spends with Manon, an independent business woman, are very interesting. She says, "There is room for both of us in our conversations. Even though we are very different, she gives me a lot in terms of listening and encouragement, and I teach her to relax, to laugh at anything and everything. (She gave a rating of 5.)

3. Clean up your relationships based on your goals. The next step is to let go of some relationships based on the goals you now have in that area of your life.

Relationship with Your Self-Esteem

Do you find it difficult to cut ties? It may help you to realize that there is a big difference between the feelings towards the people involved and the relationship itself. Indeed, you can love or appreciate a person, but the relationship may be unpleasant or not invigorating for you.

You have no doubt been improving your self-esteem for a while. If your sense of self-worth is better, you will certainly give yourself the privilege of claiming what is rightfully yours now in a relationship, no more and no less. For a relationship to be enriching, it must be nurtured by both parties; otherwise it deteriorates and affects one or the other, or both.

This is where your self-respect comes in. To what point do you endure a situation that makes *you* dissatisfied? How long will you put up with this?

For my part, I have been doing this cleanup regularly in my life for the past few years with a very clear goal: to be respected and given consideration. Let me explain. Having a generous nature, I never considered what I was getting in return from others until I focus my own needs. For example, I had family members who didn't visit me under the pretext that I lived too far away. After many years of taking one-sided steps, I made the decision to just sever ties. In my set of values, I find it inconceivable to have to explain what respect and consideration are. (I therefore give this relationship a rating of 1.)

Let me give you another example. A friend of mine would call me regularly when things were going badly in her love life and the conversation was always all about her. However, as soon as she had a new boyfriend, she would completely forget about me. One day, she called me when I was ill and I pointed out to her that she hadn't even inquired about my condition and that I didn't appreciate this complete lack of consideration on her part. From that point on, she has given me a little more attention. (I give this relationship a rating of 3.)

Now, I've learned to evaluate conversations with my "friends" and if in the majority of our get-togethers there isn't any room for me, then I realize they are talking to the therapist that I am. If I don't want to bill them as a professional counselor, then I have to take my place as a friend, voicing my needs so that I can rate our relationships with a score of at least a 4 or 5.

⊙ Forming a Support Group

Have you ever thought about forming a support group that could help you out if needed? Some people call it their *collective mind*.

One criterion to consider in these cases is to look for people you consider to be nicer, smarter or more knowledgeable than you; mentors, in a sense.

◎ Knowing How to Appreciate and Express It

If you have friends or acquaintances that you particularly appreciate, it would be a good idea to let them know *in words* how much you value them. Because whatever may be said, demonstrations of appreciation are a rather rare commodity.

One day, I heard a remark that astounded me: "The Third World is dying of starvation, while the other two thirds are dying of love." No one can change the world on their own, but everyone can improve the conditions around them in a simple yet effective way.

Do not be one of those people who, after the death of a loved one, will have regrets for not expressing your feelings to them while they were alive. By then, it is too late! Get used to showing others your appreciation now; just get started. It is never too late to learn.

I was 20 years old, in college, and undergoing psychotherapy. One of the exercises was to congratulate or make a positive comment to someone. In order to explain how hard this exercise was for me, I first need to describe my family environment a little. At home, no compliment was ever spoken, unless said mockingly or sarcastically; on the other hand, derogatory things were said clearly and bluntly. So, you had to decipher when comments were actually nice or good.

Consequently, I had never heard or directly made any positive remarks. Believe it or not, I took 60 minutes, the entire class period, to prepare myself to say this to my classmate: "Louise, you have a nice new blouse," and I ran away, red in the face … from embarrassment, as if I had just thrown an obscenity at her! Incredible, but true.

To complete my journey in that direction, life has given me the opportunity to be part of an organization based on positive recognition; I have more than once been embarrassed to receive or give encouragement. But eventually, it became second nature to me. I've even made it my job, that of a "coach," who sees people's potential and works to maximize it.

In fact, I often apply this technique with complete strangers: the cashier, the gas station attendant, or other people. If they have a remarkable attitude or if they seem to like their work, I tell them so, clearly and positively, and I encourage them to continue in this direction.

Here are some suggestions to improve your appreciation techniques:

1. Praise or congratulate people in public, and if necessary, only make reproaches in private;

2. Celebrate all successes;

3. Send written messages: It is magic!

You will feel warm connections building with the people who gravitate around you as well as forge precious bonds with those close to you. To try it is to adopt it!

✔ ASSERTING MYSELF

◎ Knowing When to Say Yes or No

If you have done the last few exercises, your self-worth probably already has a little more weight. It is only then that you can assert yourself in relation to others. It is practically impossible to determine your limits if you do not stake your own territory or recognize your own value.

Saying yes means learning to express your experiences, feelings, fantasies, ideas, and your projects without waiting for others to guess. *Saying "no"* is learning to refuse, to set acceptable limits and to enforce them, without having to give tons of explanations.

If you do not learn to say "no" when the demands of others do not meet your interests, needs, abilities or your choices, you risk living your whole life as a victim who sacrifices himself and who hopes that one day, a savior will come and say "no" for you.

Saying Yes is Also Saying No

During one of my workshops, a participant pointed out to me that when we say *yes* very or too often, it would be good to realize what we are really saying *no* to. Excellent thinking! You can do this in a written exercise.

For example:

When I say yes to	I say no to
My sister, to help her when I don't really feel like it	• My freedom • Respecting my priorities.
My boss, to do overtime at work	• Time with my family.

Go ahead and describe your own situations here. You may be surprised about what is really at stake.

Understanding Why We Say No!

In the parenting of my two daughters, I was a mother who was open-minded, permissive enough, while clearly setting the limits to be respected. In their teenage years, I changed my attitude, especially with my youngest who was the type of teen who asked for a lot, even demanding or manipulating, so I started saying no, automatically refusing any request. I did that until at a certain point, I asked myself, "Why am I saying no?"

I was entitled to a few good reasons, of course, to justify my behavior, and I found myself faced with these phantom beliefs related to my upbringing such as "A good mother must say no"; "My mother was not permissive, and I didn't kill myself," etc.

And so, I changed my mind and revised my automatic "no's." I adopted a new behavior; I would take a bit of time to think before giving my answer, whatever it might be, to make sure it was MY thought-out choice based on my daughter, and not on my mother.

As a consultant, I often see the opposite happen. Parents are strict with their children for little mistakes, they say no for no reason, and when a serious or crucial moment comes when it would be better to say no, they are exhausted and end up giving in when they most definitely shouldn't. This is called inconsistent parenting.

IMPROVING MY SENSE OF COMPETENCY

✔ **TECHNIQUES:** Knowing my abilities
Recognizing myself

◎ **Tools:** Aptitude tests
A winning resum
Self-recognition
The box of successes

✔ KNOWING MY ABILITIES

Abilities can cover multiple fields of knowledge: artistic, social, parental, etc. Here, we will specifically discuss professional skills through the application of two tools: aptitude tests and the work resume.

◎ Aptitude Tests

Part of our lack of confidence may be related to our inability to discover our innate aptitudes. One of the ways to detect our talents is to take an aptitude test. Most schools or job agencies, as well as psychologists, have them; some nonprofit associations offer these tests for free.

Personally, I am always amazed at the positive effect these reports have on my clients' attitude after they see the results. Everyone realizes that they are neither better nor worse than other people, but that they are different and unique: It is an interesting reflection of their psychological profile. All they have to do is check if they are in the right place, professionally speaking.

◎ A Winning Resume

In consultations, I have the resume, or curriculum vitae (CV), written in more of a "marketing" style than the usual standard, if you will, even for people who are not in the job market per se.

This exercise is quite labor-intensive, but it turns out to be the best personal empowerment tool I know of to nurture your sense of competency. Whether or not you hold a position or are endowed with strengths and skills, you have achieved many things, even outside of the professional sector, which can still favor your hiring or promotion; you just need to demonstrate them.

Diane has worked in the social sector for nearly 20 years. She came to consult with me because she wanted to apply for a managerial position and wanted to update her resume. The one she already had listed her education and the general duties she had at her job, with the only employer she had ever worked for in all that time. There was nothing specifying her various accomplishments.

After asking her plenty of questions, she added *all* the different roles and positions she had held. She also included all the continuing education courses that she attended. For each position, I made her become aware of her *accomplishments*. In addition, she also had a special talent as a triathlon athlete; she had competed internationally and never thought it was important to include in her resume. We corrected that, and incorporated all of this outstanding, newly revealed information.

Results? Diane felt highly valued doing this exercise and producing her new "winning" resume. As well, she was hired for the managerial position despite having no previous management experience. It was confirmed to her that her skills in the sporting world had greatly influenced the committee's decision.

◎ Self-Recognition

Since Abraham Maslow, everyone knows how much human beings have a need to be recognized, may it be personally, professionally or in any other areas; it is a fundamental necessity for our balance. However, recognition does not usually "rain down" onto our daily lives either at work or at home, so our need goes unfulfilled and can diminish our self-esteem if we do not find other ways to meet it. As the saying goes, if you want something done right, you should do it yourself!

Back in the days when hats were the height of fashion, a lady walked into a milliner's shop and browsed around. She tried on many hats and finally decided on a model made entirely of ribbons. She tries it on, seems charmed and asks the milliner for the price. "It's $150, Madam," he replies. "Seriously? You say $150, but that's really expensive, don't you find?"

Exasperated by this difficult client, the milliner takes the hat, pulls on the ribbon and thus undoes all his work. "Madam, there was only $50 worth of ribbon, the rest was my talent!"

Are you bold in your achievements or are you more inclined to downplay the result? *Being proud* of the quality of your accomplishments and accepting to *verbalize them without pretension*, these are invaluable tools to nourish your sense of competency.

◎ The Box of Successes

This is a simple tool, which some might even find simplistic. But believe me, it has earned its stripes, because for many years, I have seen it serves the "self-esteem cause" more than I have seen with some of the greatest theories in psychology. Having noticed that human beings tend to have a better memory of the "bad moves" that they make compared to the good, especially when it comes to their own abilities, I suggest making or buying a nice box in order to accumulate testimonies of your successes: photos, cards, messages, a list of goals achieved, etc.

This "success box" will allow you to gather evidence of your successes. It should be prominently displayed as a *symbol* of your abilities; please do not hide it in a closet. It is a *precious tool* to have in life's downturns when you feel as if you are not getting anywhere. During these times, put your hand inside the box and re-read those messages of love that you received from a friend, colleague or boss, or relive those feats.

I keep the beautiful greeting cards I have received in my "success box"; it is decorated with pretty butterflies, which for me are the ultimate symbols of development. I occasionally reread these free messages of gratitude from my students or my clients; it is good for my emotions, and it fuels my self-esteem. In fact, I was given another beautiful box as a gift, and it is large enough that I will not be able to overlook my sense of competency in the future.

If you do not receive any well wishes and don't know what to put in this keepsake box, I suggest you do an exercise to start feeding your box. The important thing is that you find things there that will make you smile or that will fill you with a feeling of plenty when you need it.

Exercice: Filling Your Success Box

1. To start, make an effort to remember your "good moves" at a time when you were proud of yourself. Write this down on a nice piece of paper or find a photo of this time and put them in your box. Get help from your close ones when needed. Each member of the family can have their own box. It would be a real fun and interesting conversation to have with family or friends.

    From there, all you have to do is maintain your accomplishments box, adding to it the things that you are proud of, and that you may soon forget as you go along in life.

2. Daily, take a few minutes at the end of each day to write down in your diary 10 things that you accomplished and that you felt you did well in! Do not look for grandiose events but rather all the positive things that you have done or said to someone.

And why not do it at the end of the day? It is a great time! It is better for you to fall asleep thinking about the "good things" you have done, rather than rehashing the "I forgot to… I should have … or I missed my shot, etc." This should be an essential habit, especially for perfectionists who tend to focus more on their mistakes or shortcomings.

At the end of the week, choose a few of the accomplishments that you are most satisfied with and add them to your success box to reread occasionally. You'll see that as your list grows, your sense of competency will grow as well. Here is an example of a typical day.

"My Daily Successes":

1. I did my exercise willingly.

2. I kissed my partner and said, "I love you."

3. On the road, I was courteous at least three times.

4. I gave my full attention to a colleague in order to listen to her better.

5. I made two phone calls without trying to procrastinate.

6. I managed to put the finishing touches on a file in record time.

7. I concentrated my efforts by setting aside time in my agenda for my correspondence.

8. I planted seasonal flowers in my flowerbed.

9. For dessert, I ate an apple instead of a cake.

10. I turned off the television as soon as my show was over.

At the end of the week, out of your 70 actions, choose one accomplishment that you are especially proud of. Let us say for this example, number 4. Transcribe it positively in this style: "The quality of my listening improves more and more; I practiced with Daniel and Nicole," and drop it into your success box. Someday it will make you smile to remember that you put in the effort to become who you are.

Don't hesitate to put it into practice!

SURVIVAL KIT FOR THE WORK ENVIRONMENT

✔ **TECHNIQUES:** Differentiating job and career
Promoting yourself
Recognizing one another
Preserving employee / colleague
self-esteem
Humanizing the workplace

⊕ **Tools:**   Your political sense
Meeting agendas
The Pygmalion effect
The "coaching" approach

Our professional life takes up so much of our time and mental space that it is appropriate to give it its own section in this book. Most of the information that follows concerns all types of workers. On the other hand, some of these tools may be more helpful to managers. You can also share these techniques with your boss to improve the work environment if they are not already practicing them.

✔ DIFFERENTIATING JOB AND CAREER

I approach this theme of workplace survival by distinguishing between a *job* and a *career*. In all my years of consulting, I am still surprised to meet people who confide in me that: "My job is my whole life…". I have seen some of these same people suffer from corporate reorganizations or lay-offs.

If you think of it that way, changing your perception is imperative, because a job is one thing and your career is another. You studied and chose to be a nurse, teacher, dietician, or other, it was to invest in your career and not to be employed by company X or Y. You are a nurse or teacher, regardless of who your employer is. You still have the knowledge, the expertise: in other words, the skills.

Please make the distinction! It does not change the loyalty you owe your current employer. However, you must preserve your own self-worth and your balance in this business jungle. Having a more self-sufficient and independent attitude can protect you from a serious identity crisis in the event of a sudden lay-off. A good tip? *Recognize and keep improving YOUR skills*; they will follow you wherever you go. And *know how to promote yourself*, wherever you go.

✔ PROMOTING YOURSELF

When your self-esteem is not at its best, one of the hardest things to do is to *sell yourself.* Knowing how to show yourself off is probably not a natural attitude, and your upbringing may have valued humility more than pride.

Note that I am not advocating bragging here, but rather the ability to assert yourself, which is defined as follows: "to support your dignity, your rights" and also "to put a price on yourself." If you believe that *you deserve* to be considered or promoted, you will be able to stand out without exaggeration and without feeling embarrassed.

Now that you know your qualities and aptitudes and that your resume reflects your strengths and skills, do not hesitate to show yourself off when the time is right. Know how to seize the opportunity! Gone are the days of secretly hoping that "the boss will notice your good work." These days, if Cinderella is to have her place in the sun, she has to come out of her hiding place and show herself in all her glory.

⊚ Your Political Sense

In order to promote yourself, learning to develop your political sense will be very useful to you. It is a tool that is greatly neglected in the careers of a large majority of people, often because it is unrecognized. Here are the various components.

The higher up in the hierarchy of an organization, the more political sense you have to practice. But the ordinary employee should at least know the ground rules that govern the game at hand, especially when it involves themselves, and even more so if they intend to apply for a management position. To explain this further, here are some theoretical elements of the political sense in general.

> The Definition of Political Sense

It is the ability to identify, understand and take into consideration the issues specific to an organizational environment. If you prefer, it is being able to assess the game that is going on in your department, in your company. In one type of organization, it may be like a chess match, in others, it will be an even harder game.

Political sense has the advantage of creating a dynamic environment in which it is necessary and valid because it empowers people and helps them to understand organizational issues, to be active in changing the rules, and to find ways of adapting.

> ## How to Establish Your Political Sense

1. *Have a network of both formal and informal contacts* within the company and with those who revolve around it. Do you know a lot of people? At different levels? Do you know who has the decision-making power? Do you regularly maintain relationships with them? Can you count on their support when needed?

2. *Be adaptable* in your way of saying things to the people you are talking to; this means using your tact or diplomacy in getting your point of view accepted. Are you comfortable with different hierarchical levels? Are you recognized as a flexible person? Or rather as someone who is uncompromising?

3. *Use your influence* to get your point of view adopted or to move an issue forward. Are you able to convince people? Do you use strategic arguments to demonstrate the validity of your position?

All Bets Are Off

Indeed, *having a political sense* is a desirable attitude that should normally serve the company as much as the individual who possesses it. Unfortunately, sometimes there is abuse when employees, imbued with their own success, put their personal interests first, to the detriment of their employer or colleagues. Of course, here I am illustrating a negative case.

Ginny is a dedicated employee in a thriving company. She has been working there since the very beginning with the founder. She has kept pace with the growth of the company and now occupies an important management position. The rapid development in recent years has brought new leaders, with a new immediate boss; a young man with little experience in the field, but who has a very defined career plan; he is truly career-oriented.

In fact, this new vice-president only spent about a year with the company, leaving as quickly as he had arrived, having inflicted enormous damage in terms of human resources, including for Ginny. Knowing he was leaving shortly without telling anyone, he met with her to tell her that she had no talent as a manager. Since he was in a position of authority, it literally demolished her. She had a complete emotional meltdown and suffered a burnout!

In consulting with me, we were able to identify the issues, the real causes behind this situation. Even though Ginny despises corporate politics, she is now convinced that she too has a political role to play in preserving her position at work as well as her dignity, in some way.

To make it clear to my clients who have suffered from difficult political situations, which they say "They did not see coming," I give them this mental image: "While there is a war going on in the company, the non-politicized come in to work whistling, with their fishing gear on their shoulder, while the politicized are preparing their ammunition."

The moral of this story? Political sense, in its proactive and dynamic perspective, has its place in open-work cultures and it exists ... like it or not! So it is better to know how to acquire and use it, rather than simply know how to endure it.

✔ RECOGNIZING ONE ANOTHER

Here is another workplace survival technique that involves recognizing each other, which is possible no matter what position you occupy. Even though I suggest doing this in formal meetings, this attitude can very well apply at any other time.

◎ Meeting Agendas

The purpose of a lot of meetings is to solve problems. This undoubtedly explains the glaring lack of enthusiasm of the participants who end up being tired of racking their brains for repetitive situations. Delays or absences from these meetings say a lot about the interest involved.

Of course, animating and problem-solving techniques can greatly improve the climate, and consequently, the results obtained. But there is a really simple tool that can boost the energy levels of all "possibility thinkers" looking for creative solutions.

The tool? Here it is. *Change the* meeting *agenda* by *always* incorporating a point about the positive elements achieved per team, even per individual. Some might think this is a waste of time, but you cannot ignore the human psyche. In actuality, it is a time *investment* that pays big dividends. Notice to all concerned parties!

Many companies apply this technique, especially in sales or customer service, and so much the better. But when will this be enforced for all other areas of business? Or in schools? Government? Social environments?

And if your meeting schedule really cannot allow you to add in this tool, then why not create meetings where all you have to do is discuss "good work"? I'm willing to bet that the organizational climate would be quite different... Too good to be true? Too simple to be taken seriously? Who knows?

✔ PRESERVING EMPLOYEE OR COLLEAGUE SELF-ESTEEM

Now that everyone knows how to promote themselves and recognize the success of others, we must keep in mind the importance of maintaining the self-esteem of the people we meet, whether you are a boss or an employee.

🛟 The Pygmalion Effect

In Pygmalion, a famous play by George Bernard Shaw, the professor helps a slovenly woman to become an elegant lady. At all times, he treats her like a lady, until she lives up to his expectations.

The same can apply to managers and their employees or educators with their students. In fact, a Harvard study[27] has shown, with astonishing results, that teachers' expectations directly influence student performance. At the start of the year, they were told they had "high potential" students who all achieved unexpected results at the end of the year. In addition, their intelligence quotient (IQ) had increased by more than 85%.

What these teachers did not know was that the students were actually chosen at random, not based on their potential. So, the teachers treated them *as if* they really were brilliant.

Since Goethe, it has been believed that "the only way to make a man worthy of confidence is to trust him and that the only way to make him untrustworthy is not to trust him, and let him see it." Yet, hundreds of years later, this concept has yet to be applied naturally.

Expect the best from the people you lead or simply work with! You will realize that, more than anything, it is your attitude towards people that determines the failure or success of the project in question, whether you are a manager, educator, parent or spouse.

Robert was on social assistance for a third generation in his family. He was working in a job re-entry program that I ran for a few weeks. He had managed to get a university degree in French literature and felt a little forced at having to participate in this group. He showed little enthusiasm for the work.

After eight weeks, believe it or not, he wanted to start his own writing business. I do not know if he succeeded; our paths parted ways at that point. But his transformation was obvious to everyone around him: From the loser he initially thought he was, he began to believe in his potential.

How did it happen? First, as a supervisor, I never took pity on him or made excuses for his past. I saw him as any other employee, with his strengths, his weaknesses (in his case, it was his negative attitude) and his potential. I had

---

27 McGinnis, Alan Loy (2004). *Bringing Out the Best in People.*

expected him to exceed my expectations and I placed my confidence in him. The Pygmalion Effect worked in full force.

✔ HUMANIZING THE WORKPLACE

Have you watched the film *Patch Adams*, known for its wonderful lessons in respect and love for clients in hospital settings? Among the many messages, I particularly remember the one in which he convinces the medical community to address clients by their names and not by their illness. That is recognizing human dignity.

If we make a survey into your business: Is the human resources department *human*? Does your corporate culture value its people or just results? Are employees allowed to make mistakes? Are absent employees shunned upon their return? How do they consider employees who are in "burnout"? As incapable? Or does the company admit having played a role in causing the burnout to begin with? What can you do to humanize the workplace environment a little more?

In *The Prophet*, Khalil Gibran tells us that: "Work is love made visible. And if you cannot work with love but only with distaste, it is better that you should leave your work and sit at the gate of the temple and take alms of those who work with joy. For if you knead bread with indifference, you bake a bitter bread that but half feeds man's hunger.[28]"

Be alert and active in humanizing your environment. If YOU start, it will have a positive ripple effect. Why not be the cause of an epidemic of humanity at work? This would certainly cure many occupational diseases.

☺ The "Coaching" Approach

Fortunately, management has evolved over the last few decades towards less of an autocratic style, and more of an open one, better suited to the evolution of employees who are more informed, more demanding.

One of the latest trends is called the "coaching" approach. The "manager coach" must consider the potential of their players and seek to promote greater autonomy and support for each member of the team. To do this, it must guarantee them unwavering support.

But how to implement this new management style if the managers in place themselves have interpersonal communication problems?

Be alert and active in humanizing your workplace. If YOU start, it will have a positive ripple effect. Why not cause an epidemic of humanity?

---

28 Gibran, Khalil (1923). *The Prophet.*

In my opinion, it is impossible. That is why, nowadays, leadership positions increasingly require pre-requisite qualifications related to emotional intelligence. Daniel Goleman[29] defines this by the following elements:

1. Awareness of one's emotions;

2. Control of one's emotions;

3. Self-motivation;

4. Perception of the emotions of others (empathy);

5. Mastery of human relations.

A manager with such a profile will influence the development of their employees from this same perspective. They will value the benefits of having employees with good self-esteem at all levels of the organization.

Any employee who develops their level of emotional intelligence will undoubtedly have the privilege of increasing their chances of success and will also be able to better manage their career.

Self-Esteem and Corporate Profit

What are the implications for an organization to have employees at all levels with such qualifications? Here are just a few: noticeable improvements in interpersonal communications, better creativity in problem solving, and greater ease in resolving conflicts.

Before long, research should be able to prove that these attitudes clearly translate into net profits for the company.

"COACH'S" TIP: TO BETTER INTEGRATE ALL THESE TECHNIQUES

At this point it would be VERY lucrative for you to:
1. *Reread these techniques and tools;*
2. *But especially put them to use right away: Results only come after practicing!*

---

29 Goleman, Daniel (2006). *Emotional Intelligence: Why It Can Matters More Than IQ.*

Survival And Self-Esteem

The survival of self-esteem takes different paths depending on the gender and age group we belong to. Men and women carry within them a different collective unconscious with very distinct characteristics; children, teenagers and seniors also travel very particular roads that I would like to focus on briefly. Here is the result of my reflections.

For Women

It is important to discuss the status of women in terms of their self-esteem, compared to that of men. Is it necessary to establish that religion denied for centuries that women have a soul? According to the law, women did not exist; the right to vote was granted a little more than eighty years ago. In Quebec before the 1960s, when a woman married, she would lose her name and adopt her husband's; she would become Madame Paul Saint-Pierre, for example; she could not sign any contracts, benefit from an inheritance in her name, nor sign a check or receive her salary, that is, if she had the privilege of having a job!

What about their bodily rights? The Catholic Church required women to bear children annually under pain of excommunication, and, if there was a problem with childbirth, the mother was always sacrificed for the benefit of the newborn. She could leave a widower with 10 children in poverty; it was never a question; women had no value. In our time, it is the myth of the Western model of thinness marketed around the world that influences the lives and self-esteem of a great many women[30].

Even today, some religions relegate women to second-rate roles, going so far as being denied their own civil identity. And what about female mutilation, still practiced in several countries despite campaigns to counter it? Other countries restrict the number of children per family, so baby girls have higher

---

30 André, Christophe & Lelord, Francois (2007). *Self-Esteem, Liking Yourself in Order to Live Better With Others.*

chances of being exterminated. Those are just a few examples of the forms of injustice out there.

Imagine EVERYTHING that is stored in the collective unconscious of women. This immeasurable weight that we were nothing! PHEW! You would have to agree that all of this was hardly conducive to the development of good self-esteem.

Over the last few decades, we have managed to improve the situation and to assert ourselves, at least "in principle." Young women today are not necessarily aware of the giant strides that have been made so that they have a right to "their territory," but all is not won.

In fact, equal rights have yet to come; employment equity is not a given either; the precariousness of employment for women (part-time, on-call, or independent positions) tends to increase simultaneously with the responsibilities of single-parent families which are largely attributed to women.

So many women will have to give themselves the right to exist, to reclaim their own dignity, before they are even able to enjoy the balance that comes with a healthy self-esteem.

On the other hand, if women seem to have come a long way, they have nevertheless taken gigantic strides in recent decades, thanks to their ability to open up both emotionally and intellectually. Their thirst to improve, to find the answers to get by, has brought them to all of the courses on personal growth and spirituality, to universities, indeed, wherever they have a chance to develop and learn to take their rightful place.

The new era we are entering will undoubtedly allow for a profound change in mentalities. The new women will abandon their old roles to opt for a more balanced one shared with the new men. And maybe we will soon see real gender equality in self-esteem.

For Men

When it comes to self-esteem, men have a definite advantage over the fairer sex. In general, they have a good self-image and are much more inclined to consider their personal needs. These are characteristics that women can envy them for.

Historically, in terms of dignity, men have almost always had *their* place; usually the best and the biggest one. First within the family, which calls to mind the birthright and inheritance reserved for the first-born male in a family; then, in the public sphere, where they have a monopoly on decision-making positions.

Of course, education has had its shortcomings for men too. For example, being told in a thousand and one ways that, "boys don't cry," they have suppressed their emotions so much that some now find it really difficult to share their feelings. This is where they are greatly disadvantaged and where there is undoubtedly a "malaise."

Generally, suicide rates increase progressively along with social and material inequalities. In Québec, Canada, men have higher rates of suicide in the 50–64 age group, and the overall number of suicides is three times higher in **men** than in **women**. For men aged 20 to 49, the suicide rates are lower, a trend that began in the 2000s and has continued to this day [31].

In France, more men than women commit suicide. This represents three quarters of suicide cases, and is common across most countries[32].

According to the American Foundation for Suicide Prevention, suicide is the 10th leading cause of death in the United States of America. In 2018, men committed suicide 3.56 times more often than women. Suicide rates are highest in middle-aged white men, and white men overall account for 69.67% of all suicide deaths. There is an average of 132 suicides committed every day[33].

As a general rule, it is very rare for men to seek therapy and their distress goes unnoticed. For every death, there are 100 attempts made, and 8 out of 10 men have spoken about it to those around them. The main reasons stated are they wanted to quickly put an end to an untenable situation, and to stop their suffering.

When men come to see me for self-esteem issues, in many cases it is because their self-esteem has been built almost exclusively on their sense of competency, that is, on their accomplishments. Without a job, without productivity, they find themselves without an identity.

In recent years, specific discussion networks for men have offered them avenues adapted to their emotional needs; fathers' associations also make it possible to make great strides in helping them to open up.

There is still a long way to go to create that openness in men that would allow them to better adapt to the turmoil of change. How can we adjust our educational models around them? Who will take the initiative? How do you bring up your sons? What will the men of tomorrow be? These are many questions that will need to be addressed quickly: your sons are growing up fast.

---

31 INSPQ (Québec National Institute of Public Health), updated 2020.

32 Santi, Pascale (2020). Les tentatives de suicide chez les jeunes augmentent (Increasing Suicide Attempts Among Youth), France, *Le Monde*, March 17.

33 American Foundation for Suicide Prevention: Suicide Statistics
https://afsp.org/suicide-statistics/

For Children

Notes to the Reader

I wish to make a few remarks about children's self-esteem here, but I will only just touch on the subject since many specialists have written magnificent volumes on this topic for children and their parents.

However, of my clientele of working adults, a very large proportion of them are parents. And it is inevitable when we broach the subject of their self-esteem to also discuss that of their children. They seek to promote the development of self-esteem in their children. This message is so important to the parents that I see every day that I could not refrain from mentioning it.

Even if these few pages may seem reductive, due to the short length of this section and the brevity of the techniques suggested; at least it has the advantage of demonstrating what does or does not promote children's self-esteem. It also allows me to call forth some questions from parents and educators.

In addition, I also offer any parent interested in the development of their child's self-esteem and the quality of the relationship between them, a list of specialized books that you should keep on hand for many years.

I therefore encourage you to document and obtain several of the books that I suggest to you in reference to the chapter 6 entitled: Books on Self-Esteem.

The Job of Parenting

The job of a parent is without doubt the most difficult job in the world. It lasts a lifetime without any theoretical or practical training. Think about it; What company would give such heavy responsibilities to an employee without proper training? Probably none, right?

And yet, for a parent, no instruction comes with the birth of the first child either. We learn, so to speak, "on the job." To the extent that the educational models that we have known were healthy, this may be appropriate, even very acceptable, but if they were not, we could end up witnessing something disastrous.

> *Children are not born with good or bad self-esteem; they form a self-image based largely on how they are treated by those most significant to them: their parents, teachers, their peers.*
>
> **Coopersmith**

By promoting the development of good self-esteem in your child, this will allow them to:

- Assert themselves;
- Take responsibility;
- Have goals and take the means to achieve them;
- Know that they are loved unconditionally.

Two Basic Pillars for Building Self-Esteem in Children

If we want to simplify the development of children's self-esteem to its most basic expression, it would be this: Children's self-esteem is built primarily from two pillars: **recognition** and **discipline**. Even if the definition seems simple, the constant application of these two educational attitudes is not as easy as it may seem.

1. RECOGNITION

Make your child feel secure within a reassuring attachment relationship. This starts during pregnancy and continues for many years. Being a welcoming parent, your response to the child's vital needs and your emotional presence will prove to your child how important he truly is in your eyes.

Spoil your child by offering him material things or by words alone without linking them to actions that meet their expectations and without communicating to them how much they mean to you; all of this can only harm your child's self-perception.

Because truly "*being seen and recognized*" by you and the significant people around them has a vital impact on the self-esteem that they will develop. Moreover, it is proven that the amount of love received at a young age turns out to be precious capital for the rest of their life, a foundation for self-esteem.

2. DISCIPLINE

Knowing how to set limits for children is a necessity for their mental balance from the ages of 2 to 20 years old, or almost! It is not about providing too many rules, but rather being consistent and sticking to them after you have made them clear.

It is not a question here of returning to the discipline of yesteryear, but rather to a framework where the parent remains *consistent* and *resolute* (the same principles prevail for everyone, and the parent must set an example).

This means, in other words, to be firm in your words and in the application of the rules so as not to confuse your child by acting otherwise. Better to have just a few rules and be strict in their application than to yo-yo back and forth.

In this context, these principles relate just as much, if not more, to adolescence. In fact, even if the teenager rejects all forms of rules, he still needs them more than ever. A lot of parents quit at this point (it is so demanding that it is understandable!), but tell yourself that it is *vital* to provide guidance for your young adult. We will come back to this a little later.

Favorable and Unfavorable Parental Attitudes for Self-Esteem[34]

I am pleased to offer you this table from the book *Self-esteem, a Passport for Life*, by Germain Duclos. It will allow you to understand the behaviors to adopt, and the ones to avoid, with your children.

Favorable Attitudes	Unfavorable Attitudes
Be present in a warm, welcoming way with the child	Not being physically present on a regular basis Not providing a stable psychological presence
Be reliable in responding to their needs	Neglecting to meet the needs of the child
Express unconditional love	Having unrealistic expectations
Highlight and value their successes	Ignoring their successes or not considering them important
Underline their mistakes while sparing their pride and giving them the means to improve.	Blaming them for their mistakes
Offer them a stable living environment in time and space	Not offering a stable lifestyle
Establish safe and clear rules of conduct	Not giving safe and clear rules
Be consistent in the application of the rules of conduct	Constantly changing moods when applying the rules of conduct
Be firm about certain important values and flexible on other points	Being rigid or too permissive

---

34 Translated into English from: Duclos, Germain (2015). L'estime de soi, un passeport pour la vie, reproduced with the authorization of the editor. Now available in English version (2018). Self-Esteem, a Passport for Life.

Favorable Attitudes	Unfavorable Attitudes
Impose logical and natural consequences following a breach of the rules of conduct	Imposing consequences that are too severe or that are unrelated to the misconduct, or ignoring it altogether
Reduce stressors for the child by preparing them for changes, by diminishing them and helping the child find ways to calm down when he is stressed	Showing stress in an obvious way Overestimating the adaptive capacities of the child
Be an adult you can trust	Showing a lack of openness and availability
Reactivate the memory of past successes	Ignoring the child's successes or not giving them importance
Emphasize the strengths of the child	Emphasizing the child's faults rather than their strengths
Support the child when facing difficulties	Overprotecting the child
Encourage them to find solutions when facing difficulties	Finding solutions for them
Use positive and empowering language	Using words that hurt Humiliating them and using sarcasm
Promote the expression of feelings and emotions	Suppressing the expression of feelings and needs or not considering them important
Encourage openness towards others	Be too controlling over their social relationships
Encourage generosity and cooperation	Encouraging individualism and competition
Encourage the child to make friends and deal with conflicts on his own	Resolving conflicts for the child
Give them responsibilities suited to his level	Having expectations that are too high or not high enough
Encourage them to make choices and develop their autonomy	Keeping them dependent and controlling them excessively
Encourage creativity	Ignoring or not considering the importance of their creativity
Promote their initiatives	Ignoring their initiatives or not considering them important
Respect the child's motivations	Imposing our motivations on them

Favorable Attitudes	Unfavorable Attitudes
Respect the child's developmental rhythm	Imposing early learning
Give more importance to the learning process than to its results	Focusing attention only on results
Grant the right to make mistakes	Blaming the child for their mistakes
Downplay	Imposing our perfectionism
Have fun with your child	Not making yourself available to your child. Only doing activities focused on performance or competition with them

There are many community organizations supporting parents in North America. They offer informal meetings, as well as basic and advanced parenting courses to support parents throughout their children's developmental stages. Yes! "Parenting 101" and "Teen Parenting 202" really do exist, at little cost. It is up to you to take the opportunity!

The Teaching Profession

The teaching profession has also greatly evolved through the changes in our society. The children we now welcome into kindergarten are really different from those who entered it 20 years ago. Our children today talk about AIDS, divorce or their environment, just like adults. Educational systems have practically undergone a revolution, and the actors involved undoubtedly have new roles to play.

In this turmoil of change, the fact remains that all those who have to work with children as teachers, educators or specialists, have a great interest in knowing the underlying motives that incite them to work with youngsters. Is it out of love for children? Out of a passion for teaching? Because it is their calling? Because they work 10 months a year? Because they want to provide what they didn't receive at the same age?

Beyond the activities that educators carry out with children, educational attitudes have an even greater impact on them and the educator's behaviors are intimately linked to their own self-esteem. In this field, more than anywhere else, it is crucial to be able to count on professionals who can properly manage their self-esteem.

They do not have to be perfect either, but they should be aware of their level of esteem and above all, be on the lookout to maintain the self-esteem of those they are educating. They have this moral obligation to optimally promote the esteem of the children they are in contact with. The future of our youth, and of our country in a way, depends on them.

Working with computers and hating it, or being bored shuffling papers at work, does not have the same impact in our society as being around children "who annoy us" or in whom "we no longer believe."

Teachers in Quebec represent one of the professions where there is the most burnout and it has nothing to do with their abilities. It is obvious that this profession has lost its credibility; we are far from the "master or mistress of the village" who were invested in an honorable and enviable role, or at least, highly respected. Nowadays, this profession is downright underestimated and unrecognized in its real value. Teachers will find their salvation only in their own self-esteem while they wait for the school system and parents to support them.

I would like to bring to your attention a reflection parents shared with me about our society, which they described as "*sick*." Indeed, in recent years we have paid millions to those who are responsible for our money—I am thinking here of the huge profits that banks make, for example—and, by comparison, we give a pittance to those who take care of our children in daycares. In which of your treasures would it be wiser to invest for the future … your money or your child? It is a societal choice that would certainly be interesting to debate.

A Life-Changing Observation

At 14, I was in the second year of high school (Grade 8), and the French teacher asked us to write our journal. He didn't like my first entry, and commented on what he was expecting. My second version seemed to be correct and he gave me a good mark, to which he added in writing in the margin of my notebook: "Keep it up! Quebec needs more women like you!"

At that point, I didn't understand what he meant. To me, Quebec was nothing more than the name of my province, BUT I have never forgotten that message that was intended for me decades ago. Without understanding it, he had sowed hope and had created a positive feeling within me about my potential: this teacher could see something in me that I didn't even suspect? Certainly, this simple sentence helped me to go further in life.

And If We Educated Through Positivity...

At the end of high school, my youngest daughter's French teacher asked the students to write an essay according to the prescribed rules. There was a specific theme: the importance of a high school diploma, but the point of view was left to the students' discretion.

Julie opted to defend her thesis from an ecological standpoint, ironically, arguing that the degree was of little importance compared to all the trees destroyed to produce a single piece of paper that, most often, ends up at the bottom of a drawer. This is with the understanding that most students go on to higher education, but still need a high school diploma in order to apply.

Her teacher didn't appreciate her essay at all and demonstrated to the whole class what a bad essay it was by making demeaning comments about it.

After making sure that she had respected the rules, but concerned about preserving my daughter's self-esteem, I met with the teacher to make her realize the beautiful qualities that could have been validated in the essay's style, namely: originality, creativity and nonconformity. And I raised the question that if the result was not what she expected, why was it made into a focal point, in front of all the students, to describe what a bad essay is? Why was it presented and deemed a "failure" instead of presenting an example of an ideal paper? Why not recognize the potential beyond the activity?

This experience allowed me to make a point with this teacher and show my daughter that I was supporting her in her efforts. But even more, after this incident, a few questions came to my mind: Does our school system allow children to be creative outside of the arts? Does it make children want to learn? Does it maintain their taste for life?

For Teenagers

The self-esteem of youth often takes a major turn at this point in their lives. In fact, the value they received from their parents is no longer popular, and now, to identify themselves, they will worship their friends, their peers.

Of course, it is normal for clashes to occur, and in some cases they will be more drastic. Here, in a few points, is some wise advice to get you through this period:

▶ **Guiding them;**

▶ **Supporting them;**

▶ **Supporting them without holding them back.**

▶ Guiding Them

After our teenagers have repeated the following remarks, for years, "You are the only mother ... or the only father ... who does this or does not do that," "my boyfriend's parents accept them," etc., comparing us to other parents, these young people end up doubting our abilities or our values.

In my case, it was when my daughters were teenagers that my own self-esteem was shaken. Sometimes we feel helpless; I was doubting the rules I had established. Exhausted, completely dead from repeating the same things over and over, and not knowing where to turn, I finally decided to see a specialist. At first, the school social worker reminded me of some great tips that I already knew, but had forgotten to apply, lost in all of this emotional racket.

Then, I attended a course for a few weeks for "parents of teenagers." It was a real consolation: first I realized that my parenting skills were valid; a few exercises allowed for me to have some special and interesting exchanges with my daughters. Best of all, I found that my youngest daughter had virtually no problems compared to several others, and finally, neither did I. It just goes to show that sharing often allows us to better perceive and put situations into perspective, in other words, to downplay them ... which is really useful with teenagers.

Despite their protests, it is obvious that adolescents and young adults need a frame of reference. Too many parents give up too soon due to shortness of breath. Without being rigid, one must remain firm. While taking into account individual criteria, some things are questionable, and others are not.

Adolescence is a time when our children challenge us more than ever. It is also a time to put into question our principles and our values; it is an opportunity to clean up and decide what we want to keep or what we want to get rid of. But once these conscious choices have been made, we still have to respect ourselves by making them respect us, which forces us to specify what our limits are.

Do not hesitate to consult with a professional; it can relieve you from horrible, throbbing pain. Encourage yourself by reminding yourself that this period too shall pass!

▶ Supporting Them

In adolescence, a large number of experiences occur, some of which have major impacts on the self-esteem of young people. You just have to think about the obvious, like the choice of careers, their first sexual experiences, peer pressure, bullying, violence and heartbreak. PHEW!

Depending on how deeply they react to each good or bad experience, young people will develop beliefs about themselves and build good self-esteem, or the opposite.

This is a crucial stage where the teen needs support to get through the hard knocks. Of course, they can count on their many friends who can console them for a week or two; in fact, it is rare for teens to look to their parents for that kind of comfort.

However, the beliefs they risk developing after subsequent failures can be harmful and negatively affect them for many years. Be on the lookout! Support them on their journey.

Offer to help your teens or find someone to help. Put them into contact with any of your friends that they particularly like. Refer them to serious organizations. If necessary, pay for them to consult with qualified people; your children's mental balance and their future depend on it.

Allow me to comment here on the orientation services offered in most schools. Like me, you may have encountered a large number of students who were more confused after the consultation than before. It is sad and even tragic that we are at this point. In my opinion, the problem is that we do not take the time to identify the true interests of the young person and their passions are not even touched upon. This is where the problem lies! Assessments are made on the basis of aptitude, but sometimes the correlations made with suggested careers make no sense.

Carolyn has an organized, structured personality. The first choice that was suggested to her? Joining the military. On the other hand, **Eva** always wanted to work in pharmacy, but this field is so selective that her program application was denied; her tests suggested she opts for administration. Why was she not directed towards something in, or related to, the medical field? I'm betting that she will change her education option eventually. On the other hand, **Frank** was advised to become an embalmer … for reasons that I consider obscure.

I use these examples to illustrate the point that we have to go back to basics: Who is this young person, really, full of potential and dreams? What are their interests *and* aptitudes? Adolescence is an ideal time to determine your mission in life. To get there, it requires at least three things:

1. That the young person believes that there is a place "just for them" in this world;

2. That someone listens to them and directs them according to the aspirations revealed;

3. That someone who believes in their potential and helps them discover it.

What adult, what parent do you know who pushes young people to follow their dreams, their passion?

Instead we usually hear stories like "Don't go into the arts, you'll starve" or "Go into ICT (information and communication technologies); that's where the future lies for good-paying jobs."

If more young people listened to their aspirations, if we, the adults, helped them in this direction, the next generation would probably be less likely to experience the pangs of burnout.

Nicolas wishes to study in podiatry; this training is given far from home. At this time, he is doing a bachelor's degree in biochemistry in order to perfect his knowledge base. His father does not understand this path. He keeps telling him that he is "wasting his time" because by adding up the years of schooling he "loses years of income" and that "it is money that can never be recuperated." This is an example of old-fashioned values, focused on performance instead of self-actualization.

▶ Supporting Them Without Holding Them Back

In recent years, we have come to notice that a good many young adults "are sticking" to the family nest. Some studies even go so far as to suggest that adolescence now continues until the age of twenty-seven.

Of course, the evolution of the economy may explain a certain state of affairs; the cost of living being higher, job scarcity for young people, and studies that are prolonged for many of them. But the "baby boomers" seem to be changing the rules of the game when it comes to their children, compared to how their parents were.

A poll in a daily newspaper asked the question: "Do you believe in a better future for your children than the one you have?" A very large majority of respondents said no! It is sad to be here and to believe that life will go backwards. We must certainly be the first generation to believe such a thing. This is a hint that "baby boomers" cherish their material well-being and believe that their offspring is unlikely to have the ease they used to have.

And what if that were true? Why should a young person go to a three-room apartment, which includes a microwave, cable TV, computer and the Internet? Oh yes, I forgot the cell phone and at least a four-star service[35] with their phone line?

However, there are so many lessons about the value of money and the finer things in life, young people can learn when they themselves are a bit lacking. So, they learn to appreciate. Also, student life has its bohemian side to it that today's parents have no doubt forgotten.

In my opinion, wanting to incubate our young people for *too long* risks increasing the I.O.C.: *"illusion of the omnipotent child"* syndrome[36] and undermining their independence. In a few years from now, it would be very interesting to assess the consequences of having kept the "chicks" in the family nest for too long, particularly in relation to autonomy, the capacity for commitment and accountability, among others.

Remember this truth from the animal world: Even eagles need a push to learn to fly!

For Seniors

I would also like to talk to you a little bit about the situation of seniors, because there is a lot to say and do for them, especially in terms of self-esteem. This will probably be crucial in the coming years. In fact, this segment of the population is set to increase considerably in the near future due to the number of aging "baby boomers." Beyond the number of elderly people, there are also new characteristics in this category. Having been more spoiled in life than any generation before them, and being more successful and results-oriented, these new senior risk breaking through the barrier of non-productivity with a bang.

A few decades ago, the elderly did not have the same life expectancy for that matter; at the time, it was a given that their children would keep them at home and take care of them. But that is not at all the same perspective today,

---

35 Package deals offered by telephone companies.
36 "Any traces imprinted on a child that persist in adulthood and lead them to feel that other people, in fact, the world, are meant to service their every need and desire; all in the name of love." Salomé, Jacques (1997). *Pour ne plus vivre sur la planète TAIRE (To no longer live on the planet HUSH).*

for their kids are really busy, are often geographically far apart, and most of them have no intention of housing their aging parents.

Thus, solitude or loneliness will be the number one enemy for seniors to combat against and it is only through their personal autonomy that they will be able to go through this period of life happily. *Taking charge* and *self-esteem through sharing* will allow them to survive and have a good quality of life, since for some, the retirement phase will prove to be longer than their working life.

Taking Charge

During a lecture, I had the pleasure of hearing Madame Marguerite Lescop, author of the book *Le Tour de ma vie en 80 ans (A Tour of my Life in 80 Years)*, and a very interesting and enthusiastic speaker, pointed out to us that in French, the word "vieillesse" (old age) includes the word "vie" (Life).

Madame Lescop suggested that seniors "make plans for themselves" and "just do it, without overdoing it"; this is a great recipe filled with enthusiasm and wisdom. Thus, their knowledge and experience allow seniors to respect each other, both in their choices and in their limits. This is the hallmark of wisdom!

By becoming aware of the multiple possibilities available to them, everyone will benefit from finding a *reason to live* or from setting goals for each stage of their life. Why not do the exercise every ten years: for your 40s, 50s, 60s or your 70s, etc.? This will keep you feeling "alive."

Self-Esteem Through Sharing

If there is a favorable aspect for seniors, it is that of sharing their life experience, their rich and precious past. Everyone has something to gain from this in terms of learning, pride and self-esteem, givers and receivers alike.

How can we ignore the accomplishments of various organizations that foster relationships between generations, called intergenerational; whether for social support homework or supervision, listening to music or playing pool, etc. Hats off to this initiative!

Whether it is for you or one of your loved ones, do not hesitate to promote these relationships, to encourage the older generation to invest in the younger ones or to welcome them if they come to you.

Balanced Survival For All

In short, no matter what stage of life you are in, self-esteem is an ongoing process that oscillates between the *awareness* of your strengths and limitations and *preserving a sense of your self worth.* Here is a diagram that represents its continual movement.

SELF-ESTEEM
A Continuous Process

Between

**Awareness
of My Strengths
and My Limits**

**Preserving
My Sense of Self-Worth**

CHAPTER 5

ENEMIES OF SURVIVAL AND SELF-ESTEEM

~

*The slightest wound or discomfort
can quickly worsen
and become a real nightmare,
both for the victim and those around him.
We must therefore exercise
constant vigilance...*[37]

~

37 Descheneaux, Jean-Georges (1997). *Guide pratique de survie en forêt canadienne (A Practical Survival Guide in Canadian Forests)*, p.153.

Enemies of Survival and Self-Esteem

Should you find yourself lost in the middle of the forest one day, you would certainly have to tackle several factors in order to survive: panic, boredom, thirst, hunger, cold, fatigue, and perhaps despair, among others.

As for the major enemies of self-esteem, they are undoubtedly the lack of recognition, love, and rejection that you have experienced.

In this chapter, you will be able to see how certain mechanisms function when you are injured and how they can be used to protect yourself at the same time. To survive and rebuild your self-esteem, you must become aware of your personal power and how to use it.

Life: Friend or Foe?

At the end of the previous section, I mentioned that self-esteem is a continual balancing between *having awareness of your self-worth* and *preserving your sense of self-worth*. This is still true; however, if your consciousness is distorted by significant injuries, it greatly complicates the situation.

The perception that you have of yourself was constructed little by little during your early childhood by the positive or negative reinforcements you received—whether heard or unspoken—and by the interpretations you made of them. It is by nurturing this same perception of your self-worth later on that you established the foundation for all of your behaviors.

Going back to my analogy, if you were lost in the forest, it would be much easier to find your way out if you chose to see the forest as an ally rather than seeing it as an enemy.

You could then draw on the abundance of its resources and feel replenished. It is the same with life: Far from being hostile ... life can be generous with those who learn to discover its many secrets.

Three Well-Kept Secrets Related to Emotional Wounds!

Here are three secrets related to emotional wounds. Knowing them will allow you to better understand the relationship between your emotions, beliefs and mental balance. Knowing how this process operates within you will convince you that there is something you can do to get out of it and to regain both physical and mental health. Here they are:

1. Your three bodies interact;

2. The human psyche in four stages;

3. Your trash bag.

1. Your Three Bodies Interact

Certain theories that I endorse explain that we are composed of three bodies that are superimposed in a way: the physical body, the emotional body and the energy body.

Without going into too much detail on the subject, the thing to remember is that there is an undeniable link between our three bodies which interact, one on the other, thus creating a domino effect, where one body acts or reacts to the other based on our prevailing thoughts or emotions. Besides, isn't Aristotle in 400 B.C. who said that "the psyche and the body react in sympathy with one another"? Great truths are often lost over time.

To illustrate this concept, imagine that every negative word, emotion or event that you come into contact with produces an internal wound and makes a hole in your energy body. In the long run, through suffering all kinds of physical or psychological blows, your being becomes perforated with holes, just like Swiss cheese or even a sieve. It is easy then to imagine the ensuing power outages, both physical and mental.

In addition, the more sensitive a person is, the more the blow will have a devastating effect. This difference in sensitivity, or if you prefer, *Everything that is not expressed, leaves an imprint!* resistance to pain, could very well explain the different reactions observed between two people facing the same prejudice.

As a result, a loss of energy manifests in one of the three bodies first and then bounces onto the other two. Thus, a feeling of "uneasiness" is a clue that something is going on. It's your inner voice trying to reach you! If you don't listen to it, this feeling will get worse and turn into a "malaise," more commonly known as an illness, which it does in a very large percentage of cases.

It is from this perspective that I can locate an emotion, this energy which, if it does not find release (in word or deed), will lodge itself somewhere in your physical body. That is why I often say, "Everything that is not expressed leaves an imprint!"

Any unconscious emotion will leave its mark, leave its imprint in your body, and will make its presence known through illness sooner or later. Then, based on your discomfort or your symptoms, you can decode what you are experiencing inside. A friend of mine died of a heart-related illness; everyone who knew her kept saying that she "gave of herself wholeheartedly."

It's like my comparison with the forest: Instead of visualizing illness as an enemy to be fought, if you welcome it as a friend, it can help give you a host of clues to better survive in life: you will win in the long run. Unfortunately, too many people mask these valuable symptoms with medication, alcohol and even hyperactivity.

2. The Human Psyche in Four Stages

No matter what kind of parents we have had, no child escapes certain wounds, even with the best parents in the world. So, it's important to understand the emotional cycle at the root of these wounds. This will give you a better idea of how to intervene later on in different phases of the process.

Your Inner-Self is a Magnet

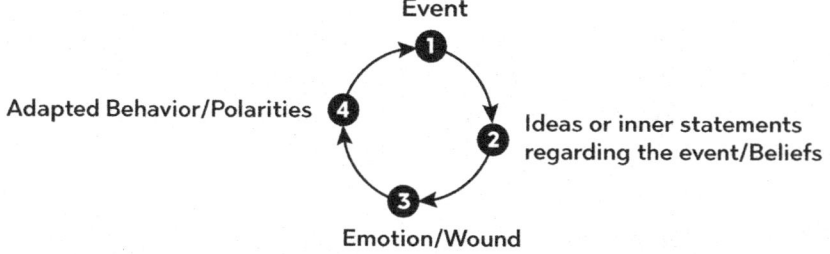

First, an event occurs (1). You get *ideas* about this event that lead you to draw *conclusions* related to this situation. Then, by repeating these ideas to yourself, a series of deep-seated *beliefs* are created (2). These beliefs make you feel an emotion that deeply affects you. This emotion inscribes itself in your physical body and can create a *wound* (3).

These beliefs forged over the years become filters that subsequently alter your perceptions of things, and at the same time prompt you to interpret reality. As soon as you say to yourself: "I believe I am like this or like that," you will then react according to these acquired beliefs (as in: "*I am worthless, I am not loveable, I am not wanted here, I am the cause of the divorce*", etc.) and to protect yourself from and survive these wounds, you will adopt certain behaviors (4) called polarities. "Polarities" refer to the two possible and opposite reactions, either passive or aggressive.

In this context, your *behaviors* will be modeled according to your inner convictions and life will then attract the corresponding *circumstances* which reinforce your beliefs because you see life exclusively through your filters. This creates a vicious circle! These are also known as "patterns" or thought processes that cause events in your life to repeat.

The drama in all of this is that the child, you were once, has grown up and that as an adult you continue to maintain these protective behaviors, even though the danger is long past. This explains some of your disproportionate reactions, at times, to situations that remind your cells of what you experienced as a child. This is why we can say that your inner five-year-old (or whatever age you were at the time of that deep hurt) is behind the wheel, and the driving force of your life. Talk about dangerous!

Let's take a classic example: a child is born into a violent household where he or she has been repeatedly beaten since early childhood. Each beating, each and every hurtful word imprints on their emotions and their thoughts. There is a good chance that this child will end up believing that they deserve it.

In terms of behavior, they may adopt the polarity of the *tough, rebellious* child, which will undoubtedly attract more violence, or they will act like a crushed *victim* which will also attract violence. Unfortunately, in both cases, chances are that as an adult, they will also repeat this violent behavior[38].

To counteract the mechanism responsible for these reiterative patterns, it is necessary to uproot the beliefs that your inner child adopted for protection long ago. These beliefs may pertain to your self-worth, love, work, money, the opposite sex, your gender, health, happiness, or whatever causes you discomfort and prevents you from having a harmonious life.

It is also true that these same events can produce very different effects from one individual to another. This is how, in the same family with the same upbringing, two children can react quite differently to the same situation. Everyone will choose the polarity which best protects them from the situation, according to their own belief system and assumptions.

Paul and Peter are two brothers who endured the demands of a critical parent, who was always dissatisfied, never acknowledging their efforts. **Paul**

---

38 Alice Miller (2002), *For Your Own Good: Cruelty in Child-Rearing and the Roots of Violence.*

became an engineer and is the president of a large and successful company. He has developed his rational side and is always results-oriented. He has become extremely demanding of his employees and is sometimes difficult to live with because of his intransigence.

On the other hand, **Peter** has rejected the "success at all costs" creed. Rather, he developed his artistic sense and became a decorator. Even though he claims to be "less emotionally stuck" than his brother, the high demands he makes of himself with respect to his artistic achievements reproduces the hold his critical parent had over him. Moreover, Peter still has the impression that, in the eyes of his parent, he still does not really measure up, even at thirty-eight years old.

Your Life Is the Reflection of Your Inner Self

You have just seen that your inner self attracts external circumstances as a magnet attracts metal. Hence, it is also true to say that external circumstances in your life are the reflection of your inner self. A common example, often seen in romantic relationships, occurs when one partner accuses the other of not loving them; it is rather that person who does not love themselves.

For more information on how the psyche works in relation to the law of attraction, there are many great books out there that will allow you to further explore this topic.

As previously mentioned, Dr. Maxwell Maltz is a cosmetic surgeon who has done extensive clinical research on self-images related to personal fulfillment. In his book, he demonstrates how self-image works in the achievement of goals: "The brain and the nervous system constitute a *marvelous and complex goal-striving mechanism*. Think of it as a sort of inner autopilot working for or against you, depending on how YOU, the operator, have adjusted it [39]".

John has great difficulty adapting to his professional life. He has had several different employers, then changed course and completely reoriented his career. However, the situation *always* repeats itself in *the same way*: he finds himself in situations where he is constantly criticized by his superiors for the way he does his work. Discouraged and disillusioned, **John** has come to despise his bosses and doubts that he will ever be able to collaborate and get along with any boss. His deep-seated belief is that "there is no place for me in the sun."

While in therapy at the age of 35, **John** identified the emotions he was feeling at this stage in his life, only to discover that they were all related to a "deep-seated contempt for himself." While searching for the causes of this feeling, he touched upon several knots[40] in his childhood linked to the fact

---

39 Maltz, Maxwell (1989). *Psycho-Cybernetics.*
40 Knot: A situation that one experiences and which causes an internal congestion.

that he was not entitled to his own vital space. He was always a "bother" to his parents who never wanted a child in the first place; they even admitted to him that he was "an accident." We can understand that it is difficult for this child with such inner wounds to believe that he will one day have "his place in the sun."

John first had to give himself the right to exist and also learn to recognize his inner beauty, even though he is not perfect. Today, he has regained his desire to live and be happy.

3. Your Trash Bag

Imagine that every human being carries a trash bag that is used to hide all kinds of unconscious emotions, instincts, hidden aspirations, etc. Say you carry this trash bag around with you all of your life. Every time you have an unconscious reaction, you put it back in the trash bag.

In his book *Apprivoiser son ombre (Taming Your Shadow)*, Jean Monbourquette does a good job of demonstrating the phases of our social development which promote this habit of subconsciously repressing some of our emotions, tastes or interests and sticking them in the trash bag. He refers to them as *black shadows* or *white shadows*, as they can be positive or negative.

Over the years, the bag gets heavy and its contents start to ferment, smell bad, and eventually explode. This is when burnout occurs, or disease develops, or depression sets in. This is the ideal opportunity to empty out the bag and clean up our life at the same time. These difficult times can also represent the chance to develop a lifesaving awareness. As Robert Bly[41] says: "You spend half your life filling the trash bag, and the other half emptying it!"

Louis is a patient, gentle man, who is easy to get along with, except when he consumes alcohol. This is when he gets angry and becomes aggressive. His aggression, stored in his trash bag, is a dark shadow. Usually, he never allows himself to express his anger except once every 10 years or so. Then he explodes in a dangerous way. Louis's aggressive dark shadow is a part of him. If he were to accept it and allow himself to express it in a more acceptable fashion, then he could avoid these unfortunate outbursts.

---

41 American poet and author.

Around the age of seven, after two years of taking piano lessons, the nuns convinced my parents to stop investing in my musical talents! At that point, my career as a musician came to an end. However, the music in me still wishes to express itself; it's a white shadow which I had hidden away in my trash bag. It has been waiting for me to take care of it, and the beautiful piano in my living room is an obvious symbol of that.

To discover this white shadow, I had to plunge my nose into my trash bag... And believe me, it wasn't always the most pleasant experience, but it was nevertheless a very appropriate and necessary step to allow me to discover new facets of myself.

Types of Self-Esteem

Dualities in Protective Mechanisms

We have previously seen that the same event can evoke different *ideas and emotions* in each individual. It is also common to observe an individual adopt completely different and opposite behaviors (polarities). Here are a few examples:

Frank has a problematic relationship when it comes to money and has had financial difficulties for years. He is well known for his "stingy" phases or his "generous" phases during which he spends lavishly.

Doris has low self-esteem. She generally feels inferior to others and frequently devalues herself; however, she is very often really pretentious when her pride takes over. She constantly alternates between these two masks.

Steven has cyclical phases in his life. At times he throws himself headlong into new endeavors until the euphoria passes, then he falls into a period of seclusion where he is no longer visible. He searches, he studies, but he cannot seem to find his true interests.

Protective Mechanisms in Romantic Relationships

Love is arguably the area of our life where our polarities are the most obvious simply because we are more vulnerable. You will be able to see the polarities adopted as a result of childhood wounds in the next few examples.

Martin and Claudia, a Damaged Couple

Martin is a businessman in his fifties, reserved but proud. As a child, he suffered an emotional injury linked to abandonment. When he returns to his home town to visit his family, he becomes very cold and aggressive towards Claudia, his wife. When things do not go his way, he holds his loved ones hostage by terrorizing them with his hysterical fits. *Little seven-year-old Martin* has most certainly been deprived of something important to him. He responded by becoming a manipulative and aggressive adult to get his way. He shows no ability to give... His polarity is to be self-centered.

Claudia is also a self-sufficient businesswoman ... except in love. In this area, she feels the absolute need to be admired by a man; otherwise, she is nothing! Born into a large family, there was no room for her except on rare occasions. To fill her inner void, she is seductive and sweet, and shows great indulgence towards Marcel. She accepts his mood swings, his criticism and his aggression. She forgives him at every opportunity, saying she loves him, but she fails to see that she is begging for scraps of affection that he obviously can't give her. The little girl in her is still "afraid to go unnoticed," yet she is now almost forty.

Danny, the Eternal Loner

Danny is an overweight man in his late thirties, who hides his fine features behind a thick bushy beard. He is very reserved and known for his gruff character and his *wild bear* style. Deep down he is a tender man who is dying to be loved, but since he believes himself to be "a monster that no one can love," he is convinced that no woman could ever be interested in him.

To prove to himself that he cannot be "loveable," he falls for the most beautiful girls around him. They, of course, hardly notice him since he is reserved or even rude, thus widening the gap between them even further. Instead of looking at women who are more likely to be interested in him, he fantasizes and dreams about rich or famous women who are all unattainable.

However, one day **Andrea**, a colleague who was part of his team, took a liking to Danny. She saw that hidden, softer part of him. They had dinner together and she was really kind to him, even showing him some affection. Danny, on the other hand, spoke at length about Josie, the most popular girl in the entire company. Andrea, who was disappointed in her failed attempt to become closer to Danny, withdrew. As for Danny, he never even realized that he had just missed his chance to be loved by an ordinary woman, a real woman who worked right beside him and who would have been ready to love him. Danny had been unable to see her because he deeply believes that love is impossible for him. He alternates between the polarities of being "afraid he will never be loved" and "dreaming of conquering the most beautiful woman" in the room.

In my case, some unspoken impressions registered during my teenage years, led me to be unconsciously convinced that my father did not love me, or rather did not love me anymore. In therapy, I came to understand the mechanisms that led me to this belief. Here they are.

When I was a child, I remembered my father's tenderness was expressed through games, tickling, and pulling me onto his lap. Then, suddenly overnight, he changed; he stopped showing me those affectionate gestures; at least, that's how I felt. This came without any warning, notice or explanation. In my mind as a young girl, I concluded that "If my father, who has no choice but to love me, doesn't love me ... then it's because I'm not really 'loveable.' So in my teenage mind, I concluded that no one else can really love me.

Many years later, I was able to cross-reference some information to explain this event which had turned out to be such a major wound. I found out that my father had been told about my first period, and he never got close to me again. The proscription of the times meant that a good father should no longer be affectionate with his daughters once they had become young women. But the inner evil was done, and the dramatic web that followed wreaked havoc for more than 20 years.

Within a few years after this feeling of abandonment by my father, I experienced my first heartbreak when my boyfriend at the time suddenly left me. Yet again, he broke off without any warning, notice or explanation.

I felt abandoned once more. I who, with the help of this relationship, had been feeding the hope of being able to deny my belief that I was unlovable. There I was, with proof once again. Twice confirmed. I convinced myself that 'loving hurts too much' and I adopted the belief "I will never love again."

My reaction was to protect myself completely behind two impenetrable layers of protection... I called them my "Pampers diapers[42]" because, at the time I learned to use these protective mechanisms, I had heard a news report on the radio claiming that this kind of diaper took hundreds of years to decompose in the environment.

I realized that I had cut myself off from my surroundings by living in my head and amputating my emotions for so many years. Unfortunately, this tainted my romantic relationships: How can we believe that our partner loves us if we are convinced that we don't deserve to be loved? It's simply impossible.

---

42 Pampers: a registered trade mark for diapers.

Impacts on my Love Life:

When I was about 16, I had a crush on a good-looking young fellow who went to my school, let's call him Norman. It happened right after my first heartbreak. We had a blast together, then about half-way through the school year, a new student arrived at school; beautiful, tall, blonde, gorgeous, and really sweet. Norman and the girl liked each other. I immediately sensed the danger of yet another abandonment without warning, notice or explanation.

Fearing this, I opted to give up my spot. I even promoted their relationship, encouraging them to go out together... What generosity, but what inner torment! This is what can happen to someone who does not feel deserving of love.

Then, my life's aspirations prompted me to want a family, so I had to find a husband. I met a man I hoped would make a great husband and father for the achievement of this goal. He indeed became the father of my two daughters. I was his shadow and he was mine. Neither of us knew how to progress in order to blend and marry our shadows. Believing that I was unlovable, I couldn't actually receive his love (because of my protective Pampers). Our relationship became more and more disappointing, until the point where I no longer had any hope of reconciliation. My deep-set belief "of being unlovable" was the backdrop for this relationship that led to a parting of ways.

Why Treat Your Wounds?

A. For Yourself First

You now understand that there is an evident and close connection between self-esteem and the wounds imprinted in you. When you are hurt, your self-esteem is distorted by your learned beliefs.

If we come back to the previous comparison between self-esteem and a compass, then your compass is out of alignment! You can no longer find "true north" or even which direction to go in, and you might even be wandering all over the place on various back roads instead of taking a direct route to get to your destination because you just cannot find your way.

This is how we take on roles (polarities), just like at the theater, to protect ourselves. At the same time, we are living a life by proxy, so to speak, rather than living our own, authentic one. Here, then, is the primary reason to heal your wounds: to find *your true self*, to be centered on **your true identity** *and your own way.*

Because of these unresolved injuries, the past remains active and alive. In fact, the contents of your trash bag ferment over the years and, at the same time, your energy reserves decrease. The situation will only improve when this endless downward spiral degenerates into either a burnout or serious illness; or else, you may wisely avoid such disastrous results with some warning now that you are able to recognize the threat. Hence the importance of treating your wounds **preemptively to preserve your mental balance** and avoid psychological and physical exhaustion.

Your self-esteem is part of you, whether it is positive or negative. It is both the consequences of your past and your foundation for the future. Therefore, your future **quality of life and overall health** depend on recovering from your past. Here more reasons to clear out those emotions that are gnawing at you.

B. For Your Children and Future Generations

Specialists in the field have differences in opinion about the repetition of "patterns" from one generation to the next. Some say that the symptoms are recurrent (Alice Miller, Ancelin Schutzenberger) and support the significance of transgenerational links and anniversary syndromes. Others, however, contend that repetition is not a matter of course and that it can be transformed into a new behavioral scenario (Boris Cyrulnik).

I, for one, tend to lean more towards the first theory and I believe that, to a large extent, repetition occurs almost automatically. Interesting researches done on two-year-old children attending day care has shown the inability of children from violent homes to show any kind of. empathy towards others: After making a brief and unsuccessful attempt to comfort and console their little friends who were crying, they ended up hitting them to make them stop[43]. In fact, they were only reproducing what they themselves had experienced in their family environment.

However, being an eternal optimist, I also believe in the possibility of salvaging a number of these cases, by means of certain factors that come from resilience[44], particularly the individual's ability to bounce back and grab hold of the lifelines in their environment that will help rescue them. An essential condition applies here: In the wounded child's environment, there must absolutely be a support system in place to ensure the means of recovery.

---

43 Goleman, Daniel (1995). *Emotional Intelligence.*
44 All of Boris Cyrulnik's book is on this topic: (1999). *A Wonderful Misfortune.*

Studies done by epigeneticist[45], Isabelle Mansuy, have shown that traumas our ancestors lived through (wars, natural disasters, etc.) are transmissible, and are visible in the genes for up to three generations[46]. This could explain a number of phenomena, including phobias, depression and a host of other problems.

Project Ice Storm: This study looked at the impact on pregnant women of the Quebec Ice Storm in Canada (1998) which affected 4 million people. Fifteen years later, epigeneticist Moshe Szyf found that these children: 1) had a significant increase in autism and asthma, and 2) their genome had epigenetic stress markers from that time[47]. Astonishing!

By taking care of your own wounds, you prevent your children from experiencing the same unpleasant situations that you went through, things that "they are not responsible for" and which contribute to generating and maintaining the same type of injury from generation to generation. I call it the *intergenerational vicious circle*. The fact is, if you do not correct this horrible emotional state, your children will end up paying for it as well.

Christian dreamed of becoming a professional athlete, but his parents refused because of the traveling involved. As a result, he was deeply disappointed and opted for a career in information technology (IT) instead. Today, he pushes his own son to the limit in sports, just so that he can realize his own disregarded and buried dream. At first glance, Christian's actions could be described as laudable, but he should nevertheless give his son the chance to choose for himself.

Monica was mistreated as a child. Beaten and denigrated, she suffered a great deal and swore to herself that her children would never have to endure such things. One day, feeling distraught and helpless because she could no longer bear her 20-month-old baby's incessant cries, she nearly exploded. Before doing something she would regret, she phoned a helpline for parents in need. She was listened to and offered help. She now knows that she has to go through an inner healing process to free herself from the domestic violence she experienced and to make sure her child is safe from this transgenerational defect.

---

45 Refer to chapter 7 for the definition of *epigenetics*.

46 Her article (2017). "Transgenerational Epigenetic Inheritance: From biology to society."

47 DNA Signature Found in Ice Storm Babies- Douglas Mental Health University Institute. http://www.douglas.qc.ca

Surviving
in Stormy Seas

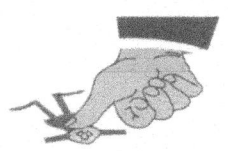

You probably understand why it is relevant to treat your inner wounds, but that doesn't necessarily mean that you have the strength to do so.

When you hear people saying "For years I was in survival mode," they are either referring to difficult years financially, or psychologically painful times in their life where they seemed to have lost control. It's a little bit like swimming faster just to stay afloat because you feel overwhelmed, as if you are about to be submerged by a giant wave.

There was a time, specifically a few months after my divorce, when I felt as if I was sagging under the weight of this failure in my life. Every morning when I walked into the office, I felt like a puppet hanging on by one string that I felt was connected to my head. I still remember the color of the carpet; it was a dull gray. Every morning I was afraid that I would fall into this gray sea, until one day, so overwhelmed and at the end of my rope, I almost wished I were lost in it.

Despite my dismal condition, I could still function professionally but I wouldn't question my wounds; I didn't even have the energy to think about it anyway. I finally took a few days off at a health center, which allowed me to catch my breath and replenish my energy level, at least for a while.

Once I was physically back on my feet, I was able to see my situation more clearly, but I felt paralyzed. It took the help of a friend to nudge me in the right direction and get me to seek therapy. It was from then on that my search for myself turned to the holes in my self-esteem.

Dead End: It's the End of the Road!

It may have happened to you that you knew exactly where you were, that you were at the end of the road, a real dead end, with no possible way out. From your point of view, you were probably right, but might there not be other ways of looking at the same situation?

For example, you are lost in the middle of a forest, and you are stuck at a dead end. If a plane were to fly over the vicinity, its pilot would certainly see that you are actually stuck *on the trail where you are now*, but they would also be able to assure you that there are other paths all around that you could be taking; you just can't see them from your location.

However, if you do not believe the pilot, or you think that a rescue effort is not for you, if you are convinced there is no way out, you will simply not find any.

In the same vein, based on what is being written on the subject these days, one has to wonder if suicide has become ... a life option. Now there is talk of "succeeding in committing suicide." When stars or famous people decide to end their life, there is all this media hype about trying to justify their desperate gesture, which often triggers a wave of suicides in the population.

More and more, we are unconsciously instilling in our youth that ending their life is a possibility, and this is happening at an earlier and earlier age. Now children have access to this notion by watching cartoons on television where the hero is being chased and becomes caught at the end of a cliff, with no means of escape and with no other alternative than to jump...

When there is no one around to re-establish the facts or to direct them towards other choices, how can we be surprised that suicide among youth is more and more prevalent?

The only thing to do when you are stuck at a dead end, in life or on the road, is to BACKUP... UNTIL YOU FIND ANOTHER WAY OUT! At least make this last effort. Please do not go any further; you are headed straight for the edge, and if you don't even have the strength to retreat, then call for help!

Your Ability to Adapt

"Our body has the gift of " *adapting* to any crisis. It also has the ability to *obey our will* and accept any progressive training we impose upon it: muscular, physiological, psychological and social[48]."

At the same time, on a human level, when our personal challenges overwhelm us, these two factors also play a very important role in helping us to adapt. Victor Frankl, a Jewish psychiatrist imprisoned in the concentration camp at Auschwitz, confirms in his accounts that one of the factors that allowed for the survival of many detainees suffering the horrible conditions at Auschwitz was the power to visualize the future. This ability to anticipate events in the future, to hope, saved many lives.

Are you a Pike or a Flying Fish?

An impressive documentary featured the "pike syndrome," where a human behavior specialist wanted to demonstrate the ability to adapt to situations. In the center of an enclosed pool, a pane of glass was installed where the pikes would hit into while swimming. After a while, the glass was removed and they observed that the fish would not go beyond the limit previously set by the glass. Likewise, human beings often mold themselves to the situations they are experiencing and end up not being able to see beyond the obstacles. Even when there are no more barriers, they also do not attempt to cross the line, just like the fish.

But then there is the flying fish who jumps out over the water, differentiating itself from the pike. It is this sense that Boris Cyrulnik speaks of psychological resilience[49], which he defines as "the ability to succeed, to live and to develop positively, in a socially acceptable way, in spite of the stress or adversity which normally involves the serious risk of a negative outcome." Cyrulnik has studied many cases of war survivors or victims of crime who have managed to live a serene and happy life, despite these significant and traumatic life experiences.

Which category do you fall into? That of the pike? Or the flying fish? Know that there are always other possibilities... All you have to do is to look further, above the obstacles, beyond the limits that are holding you back.

---

48 Maniguet, Xavier (1994). *Survival: How to Prevail in Hostile Environments.*
49 Cyrulnik, Boris (1999). *A Wonderful Misfortune.*

The Will to Survive

In order to survive, you must first have the will and the desire to do so. What is your taste for survival? Why would you make the effort to get through overwhelming situations? Who or what motivates you?

One summer, at a particularly difficult, even pathetic time in my life, I cried for days on end. As if it wasn't enough even then, time was going by too fast; I still had this well inside that needed to flow out of me so I could empty my sorrow. Then one day, I had had enough; the idea occurred to me to let go, just drown in my tears and die: "It would be such a relief," I thought to myself, a release. I was on the brink.

But at that moment, I felt a whole new rush of energy growing inside me, pushing against my thoughts, as if lifting my body off the couch. I felt that part of me that wanted to come back to life, to live, period. Then the faces of my two daughters appeared in front of me, giving me my true reason to hang on. I held on to life; I rebuilt myself, slowly reconstructing, step by step, one day at a time.

Distress Signals

Generally speaking, to survive in the wild, there is an array of internationally recognized distress signals, such as the Morse code, body signals, signaling mirrors, and so on. It is unfortunate that there are no clearly established distress signals for everyday life. The only thing left for us is to become more open to others and to seek help for ourselves.

However, since there are no pre-established signals, there is a good chance that you will have to repeat your own signals over and over again or to more than one person before they are heard or understood. Just try to be clear and simply say, "I need your help!"

CHAPTER 6
PERSONALIZED FIRST-AID KIT: HOW TO REGENERATE YOUR SELF-ESTEEM FLOWER

~

*Aim for maximum efficiency
and minimal futile efforts.*[50]

~

50 Descheneaux, Jean-Georges (1997). *Guide pratique de survie en forêt canadienne (A Practical Survival Guide in Canadian Forests)*, p.202.

Personalized First-Aid Kit

We have seen that self-esteem can be devastated by deep wounds that may have been present for a long time. All the tools previously mentioned can support you, of course, but to continue going deeper and further, here are a few more that can help heal your soul.

I will emphasize, however, on the essential condition to healing: You must take the first step and recognize that only you can heal yourself; the doctor or the therapist is only there to accompany you.

Give yourself a reasonable timeframe, say a few weeks; if you have not succeeded in taking charge of your healing process, seek help first from a doctor or a therapist.

Accept That You Are Responsible for Your Own Life

No matter the kind of past you've had in the form of impossible parents, traumatic experiences, wounds that have left scars, and no matter who you have blamed until now, as of today, the problem is all yours!

Only you can now decide what the rest of your life will be like! Your future depends on your thoughts, your emotions and your actions TODAY. You only have control *over the here and now* and yourself alone… certainly not over others.

In order to do this, you must have a clear awareness of your past. You must then make a clean sweep of it and start on a fresh path. As Jacques Salomé once said: "*The more I take care of my needs, the less I need to fill my voids!*"

Your ability to positively envision the resolution of your problems and to **actively** look for creative solutions instead of complaining or feeling sorry for yourself will be

> The more I take care of my needs, the less I need to fill my voids!
>
> **Jacques Salomé**

really useful in undertaking your personal healing process. It has been proven beyond a shadow of a doubt that a positive mental attitude has a better effect on physical and psychological healing than a pessimistic attitude. This has nothing to do with the "magical thinking" referred to by psychologists, in which events resolve themselves magically in a snap without any effort or intervention of any sort, a theory I do not believe in either.

First-Aid Kit
for Self-Esteem

Here are a few things to consider that will help you take better care of yourself and which should be part of your first-aid kit when those feelings of uneasiness start to grow, or even when your inner voice tells you that you are off balance.

For those small hurts, you may feel from time to time, these are the equivalent of aspirin, iodine or a Band-Aid strip for cuts and scrapes. The following three exercises are comparable to the effect of an antidepressant, on condition that you use one or the other of them daily.

◎ Recognize Yourself Every Day

Taking time to care for yourself (at least fifteen minutes per day) will help you treat the wounds of the heart as they occur. Treat yourself today, tomorrow and every day! How? Make a list in advance of things you like, make up a menu of what pleases you, so that just like at the restaurant, you can choose something "à la carte" every day.

You can set aside a time every day to do a few exercises pertaining to one petal of your self-esteem flower. Go back to chapter 4, Survival Kit, to make use of the tools there.

◎ Your Box of Successes

Take your "success box" out every day. If you have made sure to fill it with your successes, you will realize its usefulness in dealing with disappointments or brief sadness or even in times of great distress.

If you do not have your box of accomplishments yet, make one and use this exercise as the first step toward healing. Ask for help if you need it.

⊚ "Be Good to Yourself"

Here is a good mental exercise. Use your imagination and creativity to rid your mind of today's source of pain and to be caring and tenderhearted to yourself.

Learn to be "good to yourself," indulgent, less demanding, less of a perfectionist. It did not go the way you wanted it to at work? And ... so what? It will be better tomorrow. You are disappointed in yourself? All is not lost; it is not the end of the world! Stop beating yourself up about it.

The Exercise

Lie on the couch or settle comfortably into your favorite chair: relax. As you relax, take a few deep breaths. Empty your thoughts and proceed as follows:

1. Choose the situation that you wish to review for that day or the unpleasant emotion you would like to get rid of;

2. Be lenient with yourself, welcome yourself into the situation as you would be for your best friend by minimizing his or her failure or painful emotion. Downplay the situation;

3. Imagine then, the new scenario: revisit the event from an ideal perspective, as you would have liked it to happen, and give yourself the starring role. It doesn't cost anything to dream!

4. TASTE that moment, and savor it! Don't forget, your brain cannot tell the difference between a real situation or an imagined one: it imprints and then attracts it.

By doing the following exercice almost every day, it helped me to distance myself from the less satisfying results in my life, to be less hard on myself and accept, with some wisdom, that for every human being, things are not always great every day of your life, as is the case for me. It's important to be realistic and keep the faith: high tide always follows low tide. Such is life!

> Your brain cannot tell the
> difference between a dream
> situation and a real one.

First-Aid Kit
to Treat Deep Wounds

For deeper, more serious wounds, that are at the root of your "patterns," or that have made you physically or mentally sick (a burnout or depression), it is easy to understand that healing and rehabilitation cannot happen overnight. You will have to *invest* and be the co-creator of your own health. I sincerely wish you the courage to *seek professional help* according to the needs of your situation; doing so will greatly shorten your convalescence.

✔ **TECHNIQUE:**   Become aware of my discomfort

◎ **Tools:**   **Writing and rereading**
                     Talking of myself

✔ BECOME AWARE OF MY DISCOMFORT

When you are at the end of your rope and you explode, it does not matter if it is at the office or within your personal relationships, you normally wonder how you could have reached such a point and blown up in that way. One of the obvious answers is that you were not listening to the first signs of your "uneasiness." Something was bothering you, but you did not listen to your inner voice whispering in your ear about your discomfort in that particular situation.

After the fact, you remember the feelings you tried to hide behind logical reasoning. Remember: *what does not express itself, imprints itself,* whether we like it or not. That is why it is more and more important to be aware of your inner life.

The goal of this process is to succeed in healing your inner wounds. The starting point is to *realize that you are suffering*. Otherwise, what is there to treat? What is there to cure?

The following steps will be *to express* these feelings, either verbally or in writing and to go further to really *understand* what's involved, to see the relationships between the different elements. It is only at that point that you will be able to *act and heal*.

Claire experienced a difficult situation at work when she was demoted. This change really upset her, first in so far as the type of work and second because of the resulting humiliation she suffered. By putting into practice a series of meditation exercises, she succeeded in getting over this professional failure and it helped her diminish the intensity of the pain she experienced. The problem was that she kept denying her pain and stifling it.

Fifteen years later, she came to see me because she wished to reorient her career and start her own business venture. Her plans, however, were not working out. The process we undertook together helped her heal the wounds related to the event that had imprinted within her those negative beliefs about her professional abilities and her right to be successful.

⊚ Writing

Writing is also a wonderful tool that is too often forgotten or at least neglected. This is unfortunate because it is an useful form of expression. Without necessarily keeping a diary—which is, by the way, very valuable, but requires a lot of effort—try, at least in the toughest or most chaotic moments of your life, to write down, over a period of a few days, the thoughts that come to you and the emotions that are upsetting to you.

Even in books on wildlife expeditions, it is suggested to write, to take notes when lost in the forest to have some point of reference and be able to figure out what to do. By the same token, writing down our observations about ourselves helps us to *be aware* of our current position. This is why writing is so important on your road to self-discovery.

What to Write About and Why?

Writing down your emotions, your states of mind might help, first of all, to relieve the internal pressure that can get to you at times; it's a bit like a **safety valve**, whether it be:

- An event you have lived through;
- Your beliefs;
- A subject you feel strongly about.

Writing to Vent Feelings of Anger

When events provoke anger, rage and resentment within you, they are important opportunities for you to express your emotions: this means taking the emotions out of your head or body by verbalizing them or writing them down.

When these situations occur, you must write EVERYTHING that is going through your mind, no matter what order, what vocabulary, what level of language or what adjectives you ascribe to your (absent) counterpart. Let your anger and aggression flow out of you ... and onto the paper.

Do this exercise a few times, if necessary. When you feel you have completely vented the emotion, destroy the papers. You can burn them; it's very good, symbolically, for putting an end to the situation and purifying it. It is important to destroy the papers for real; otherwise, you are imprinting these negative emotions even more so in your life.

You will see that anger is *an emotional* screen that hides other emotions: keep digging and searching as far as you can to identify the real feelings that are involved here.

Writing to Provide Clarity

Sometimes, we have to stop just to *understand* our reactions. If you are deeply troubled by a situation, take a few minutes to determine what is going on and to untangle your bundle of mixed emotions.

A few years ago, my ex-sister-in-law died. She was in her early forties and I had known her for over 20 years, I was attached to her. So I went to the church for her funeral. Less than an hour later, I was driving away with anger in my heart. I ranted and raved the whole way back.

Once home, I warned my partner that I was not prepared to go out as we had planned, nor was I ready to talk about it. In fact, I asked him to give me half an hour to write. It was sufficient for me to untangle the numerous and strong emotions I had experienced during that single hour. In the end, all my anguish was dissipated.

What Is Your Monologue ... Or Rather Your Soliloquy?

A soliloquy is the inner monologue that you maintain with ... yourself. It's the secret spontaneous thoughts you alone can hear. Sometimes you express them verbally, but quite often, you don't dare tell them out loudly, especially when you're denigrating yourself.

And yet, it is so important, even vital to your sense of balance, to really understand your soliloquy, to become aware of the true nature of your thoughts. This will allow you to either change them, as needed, or nurture them if they satisfy you. They reflect your beliefs.

It is always possible for you to lure others by hiding your vulnerability, but it would be the height of unconsciousness to want to make a game of dodging your own thoughts. But alas, that is often the case!

So here is a writing exercise, in which you have to answer, as spontaneously as possible, what you think about the following topics. You could redo the same exercise on different occasions to compare your answers. Open up your expedition journal and start free writing.

MY SOLILOQUY ABOUT:

My successes?

My efforts?

The compliments that I receive?

The insults that I take?

The beautiful things that happen to me?

The hard knocks that occur?

My failures?

⊙ Reread

Then READ OVER what you wrote; that's the key to the technique! Sometimes, by re-reading your writing afterwards, it will allow you to detach, somewhat, from the situation, and you will be able to see it from a wider perspective. Then, you will know better where you are at; you will be more capable of reorienting or recentering yourself.

Isabelle had been writing in her journal for a long time. However, she never read over her own writing. It is only years later that she found her book again and read what she wrote about during a certain period of her life and her friendship with a colleague from work. By re-reading it, she came to the following conclusion: "I was really in love with that man and didn't realize it then! If only I had read over my journal then, I would have understood myself better: Reading about it made it so … obvious!"

◎ Talking of Myself

Though writing can be really useful, do not forget, however, to verbally express what you are going through. Sometimes, by expressing a situation out loud, we really hear ourselves … and we often find a solution rather than turning things over and over in our mind.

Open up to a friend whom you really trust; it will help you to see more clearly. Feeling like we are heard can sometimes be enough to give you the momentum you need. In many cases, no one can do anything for you, but the mere fact of feeling supported or appreciated for what you are going through is like a refreshing balm on a wound. Moreover, you may be lucky enough to have someone that gives you sound advice and enlightens you through his or her perspective on the situation.

Here is your chance to verify your willingness to take your rightful place, by asking yourself these two questions:

- When I have a problem, do I give myself permission to talk about me?

- *Or do I minimize the effect of the situation "because I feel as if I'm not important"?*

I consider myself a talkative person, but rarely do I talk about my personal concerns, even to a friend. I was, however, happy to confide in my therapist because it was not threatening for me. I could show my vulnerability without fear because after the consultation, she would not be part of my life.

During a week-long intensive training course in psychology, I realized my tendency to be reluctant to open myself up on a personal level. Confident in my ability as an animator, I often offered to play that role in the team, which allowed me to talk last if there was time remaining… A teammate saw what I was up to and had the roles changed as well as the speaking order! He got me alright! All this because I didn't recognize the benefit in having MY place and taking it.

Talk... Even if You Don't Have Any Friends

The mere fact of expressing yourself in stressful situations is still a valid step that is reassuring and very beneficial, even if you don't have a real friend.

In moments when you feel isolated from others, without anyone you can really trust, there are still help lines with specialists who are waiting to take your call. Reaching out could be useful, even lifesaving. Don't hesitate!

✔ **TECHNIQUE:**   Controlling my thoughts
                    Mental programming

◎ **Tools:**   Your words: a magic wand
                    The gift of a parrot

✔ CONTROLLING MY THOUGHTS

It can seem strange at first when I talk about *controlling* your thoughts in a situation of emotional survival. On the contrary, think about it: whether you practically fall into a panic because your boat is sinking into the sea or you are in despair at having lost your job, a key to survival is to *manage* the flow of ideas or images going through your mind. It can sometimes mean life or death.

Regardless, let's say that thoughts can be considered on three levels: ❶ Automatic thoughts, either verbal or visual *soliloquy*; ❷ More durable cognitive reasoning; ❸ Premises, values and beliefs that make up our fundamental structures.

During private consultation, I have seen numerous cases of clients with poor self-esteem that maintained a negative soliloquy about themselves, using self-deprecating messages. Of course, we can find the root of those self-esteem problems in childhood, we can take care of the emotional scars, but at the same time, we have to put an end to the self-destructive process of our own thoughts once and for all. Once they have been acknowledged, it is absolutely essential to prevent them from causing further damage.

Nourish your faith and your doubts will die of starvation!

"*Nourish your faith and your doubts will die of starvation!*" I don't remember where I first heard that sentence, but for many years, it has served me very well to stay focused on what I want rather than center my attention on what's wrong. Keep it in mind and post it when needed.

Controlling our thoughts is not an easy job, particularly if we come from a negative, violent or denigrating environment. The more recorded mental messages are "infected," the more work there is to do, in quantity as well as quality, to disinfect them.

However, knowing certain key elements will certainly make learning that control technique easier. ❶ First of all, you can't think about two ideas at the same time; ❷ Secondly, there is only one person in charge of your mind: YOU; you are the only one that can ensure the control of your thoughts. ❸ Furthermore, everything learned can be unlearned, and everything programmed can be reprogrammed.

Controlling our thoughts doesn't cure the emotional injuries by itself, it only prevents gangrene from setting in. This allows you to stop hemorrhaging energy—if I can use this metaphor—caused by denigrating, defeatist and negative thoughts.

"Positive thinking" contributes to healing such as chemotherapy does with cancer, but positive thinking, purely and simply, cannot heal deep wounds whose causes have to be extracted by the root so that they do not grow back again as cancer does.

In all my life, I have never met *a wholly negative* person, who was convinced about failing and ended up being wrong about the anticipated results! So, I prefer to continue sharing what a Quebec comedian claims: "It's better to be rich and healthy than poor and sick!" and look forward to succeeding.

Exercise: Mental Training

This exercise will serve as basic training for learning to manage your mind. Once this step is mastered, you will be able to apply other methods to reprogram yourself depending on what you choose.

1. THINK ABOUT A NEGATIVE IDEA OR FEELING OF POWERLESSNESS.
   Close your eyes and begin to think of one of your feelings of powerlessness. Repeat it many times in your head. Note the effect it has on you. For example, "I am good at nothing, I am unlucky."

2. PUT A STOP TO THIS IDEA: YELL, "STOP."
   Mentally yell "stop" to that thought or "CANCEL" if you prefer.

3. REPLACE IT WITH A POSITIVE OR POWERFUL IDEA.
   Immediately change your thought to a positive one. If the negative idea comes back, once again, yell "STOP" or "CANCEL" and refocus your attention on the positive thought. No matter how many times your negative thought comes back, refocus your mind repeatedly on

your strength, again and again. Note also what you feel. You can start the exercise over for each one of your negative thoughts.

4. BE VIGILANT.

   After this intensive session that has taught you to train your mind, pay attention to your thoughts. Each time you catch yourself thinking about something that makes you feel powerless, yell "STOP" or "CANCEL" to yourself and focus on your strengths. Develop this reflex. Can anyone think for you? It's up to you to stay in control!

When I began practicing this exercise many years ago, in a difficult situation where fears haunted me, I had to do it at least one hundred times a day at the beginning... Yes... You have read correctly, a hundred times every day. I had a lot of work to do to control my fears.

Then, I was able to "stay in control" more and more and it has become automatic for me now. When I say "CANCEL," it brings me back to a position of strength.

✔ MENTAL PROGRAMMING

New mental programming serves to either change or maintain our inner thoughts. The soliloquy we are used is like a looped voice recording that plays the same content over and over again in our mind. It's like an old computer program that needs to be updated; it has to be reprogrammed.

The technique is much more effective if you have healed the source of your wounds and identified negative beliefs that have come from them. This programming consists of repeating sentences that replace the inner erroneous or destructive soliloquy. Here are some tips to optimize results:

❶ Use "I" (You can't program someone else);

❷ Use the present tense: "as if you were or already had" the desired characteristic and;

❸ Include the expressions "more and more" or "better and better" which often facilitates a more acceptable progression for your little inner voice. For example: "I am more and more assured in my decisions. I take the place that's allotted to me and people appreciate me more and more".

I have to emphasize, once again, that if you try to program ideas that are contrary to your deepest beliefs, **your inner beliefs will win out** and the programming won't allow you to reach your objective, **even if you were to repeat the new program a thousand times a day.**

For example, someone creates the following program: "My physical and mental health improve from day to day." Even if this person notes some actual improvements, he or she won't be able to recover excellent health if their profound belief is that "it's more acceptable to be sick than to fail professionally, because sickness is socially acceptable but failure isn't."

Here is another example of faulty programming from a financial standpoint: The pattern "I am financially independent" repeated millions of times by someone who has the deep-seated belief that he or she "doesn't deserve to succeed," will accomplish almost nothing. If, moreover, there is the conviction that "one has to work hard to succeed," that person could invest superhuman efforts and never achieve the desired results.

◎ Your Words: A Magic Wand

Once we begin to notice our inner thoughts, it's essential not to contradict ourselves by saying things that would completely cancel our programming. Therefore, be careful what you say because your words are like a magic wand! They can work in a positive or negative way.

The speaker at a lecture once said, in a similar vein, that "one is hung by one's tongue," meaning that by continuously repeating the same refrain, it ends up happening in our life. Of course, it doesn't happen instantaneously or by magic, but it takes shape with time. It's well known that people who believe and say they are lucky end up that way, and so do the discontented.

◎ The Gift of a Parrot

To help you to keep your self-talk in check, I am offering you this special tool and calling upon your imagination. For many years now, I carry around on my shoulder, a magnificent, colorful parrot; it helps to remind me when my self-talk is not up to what it should be… Every time I talk to myself, it cuts me off and simply asks: "Is that really what you want?" It acts that way simply to confirm if what I have been saying to myself really corresponds to what I think and hope for myself. That dear Peter-the-Parrot, caught me off guard at first, but it eventually helped me to rectify my self-talk, so that I now only think of things I really want to attract.

During my workshops, after having explained this, I always enjoy observing the ongoing discussions during the break. In an attempt at humor, I will often interrupt participants suddenly asking them in my best parrot voice: "Is that what you really want?" It is surprising to me how often people realize how negative their self-talk can be.

This helped me so much, I am now offering you a wonderful parrot, in whatever plumage you like. Which shoulder would you like it to perch on? There you go, but be very careful what you wish for yourself in the future ... your parrot is watching you!

✔ **TECHNIQUE:**   Managing my emotions

◉ **Tools:**   Tenderness
   Psychokinesiology

✔ MANAGING MY EMOTIONS

Some therapies teach us that by simply confronting our emotions and rationalizing them, we then succeed in controlling them. This approach certainly contributes to our quality of life, but only to a certain extent. At the very most, it will last until the next event that places in a situation that sets off an intense reaction that reminds us of a similar event from our past.

In my opinion, the best way is to identify the deep, underlying causes of our emotional wounds, and heal them, the same way we would weed out a garden. *Tenderness* is the golden thread, an almost fail-safe recipe for thoroughly healing our emotions.

◉ Tenderness

Tenderness is a real effective remedy for many chidhood wounds or discomforts[51]. To use it, all you have to do is imagine a small child standing by your side that you are caring for with all the love and tenderness he or she deserves; that child is you at the age of 2, or 4, or any other age you might choose.

Speak to the child in silence or out loudly, rock them or take them out for ice cream. Spend the day with them. The important point here is to give the child what it is that they missed at that particular age, to tell them the things he would have liked to hear, to comfort them if needed.

---

51 The basis of that theory comes from John Bradshaw's book *Home Coming: Reclaiming and Healing Your Inner Child*, 1992.

Using the Spontaneous Method

You can do this at any time. Find a picture of yourself when you were young. To begin, choose a difficult situation you remember going through or that was mentioned to you as having had a significant effect in your childhood.

Show love and tenderness to the child and speak to them, telling them *exactly what you would have liked to hear to avoid being hurt. Put your arms around them and rock them if needs be.*

You can heal your inner child and replace all of the negative messages from your childhood with positive acceptance, tenderness and validating messages. You will reclaim your right, and choice to be truly loved. Why not opt for an *overdose* of love for a few days?

⊙ Psychokinesiology

Modern equipment can help us find magnetic north. The same goes for psychology. A modern technique was developed and has proven to be successful in finding the exact causes of our "uneasiness" and our diseases: It's called psychokinesiology. I would like to explain this technique in which I was trained[52] and through which I was able to help many of my clients find their "*joie de vivre*" and accomplish their life goals.

It is an **efficient, targeted** approach used to heal our wounds and break the repetitive cycle of rejection and hurt. It is also called the science of tenderness.

Psychokinesiology is the synthesis of numerous sciences and disciplines, such as Chinese energetic medicine, applied kinesiology and different psycho-therapeutic approaches. The muscular test, usually done on the arm, is as accurate as a compass that directs the practitioner to the answers imprinted within the body. I have seen proof of this hundreds of times.

This technique includes three premises:

1. Our body has a cellular memory which remembers all the events from birth to the present day. Psychokinesiology uses this priceless data bank to heal the body and spirit.

2. Our body does not lie. Case in point: Have you ever tried to stop shivering when you are cold? Stop shaking after a shock? Our body language is used as a therapeutic tool.

3. The body automatically heals itself.

---

52 Lévesque, Aline & Flückiger, Hedwidge (2003). *La tendresse: chemin de guérison des émotions et du corps par la psychokinésiologie, la science de la tendresse (Tenderness: path of healing emotions and the body through psychokinesiology, the science of tenderness).*

A Complete Session

Here is how a psychokinesiology session is conducted.

First, the client goes to a therapist's office for all kinds of reasons; with psychokinesiology, you can test everything: physical or psychological problems (anxiety, stress, self-esteem, etc.). The therapist asks a series of questions, consistently applying a specific technique, and using the client's arm, the therapist will find the exact, and often surprising answers.

During this type of session, we can:

- **Find out** in which organ the negative emotions are lodged in;

- **Identify** these emotions (fear, anxiety, anger, etc.);

- **Determine** precisely at what age these negative emotions were imprinted within the body;

- **Retrace** the events that caused these emotions;

- **Heal** the inner child by naming the wounds and by adopting them. The act of healing resides within the heart: that is what heals!;

- **Verify** the negative beliefs acquired as a result of these wounds;

- **Re-program** a set of new beliefs by associating them with today's reality.

The limits we impose on ourselves are often just simple beliefs. That is why it is crucial for us to find the roots of our limitations and modify them so we can realize our full potential. Psychokinesiology is a fantastic personal development tool with which to transform and heal.

A Few Cases

Ariel is a consultant who had to give a training session during a convention. This new assignment was a source of tremendous stress for her. She came to see me because she had sharp pain in her neck and shoulder; in fact, the pain was so severe she could hardly raise her arm. She believed the stress was directly related to the training session she had to give. It reminded her of a time she had to speak in front of her fellow students when she was in college and remembered the humiliation she had felt at the time. This explanation seemed plausible.

I offered to use psycho-kinesiology on her to find out what was going on. She accepted, saying that we could give it a try but insisting that she had no recollection of her childhood prior to the age of six.

With the help of the muscular test, we identified a feeling of sadness lodged in her lung which was directly linked to an event which occurred between her and her father at age 4. After a few minutes, she suddenly remembered and told me the story. Her parents were packing boxes to prepare for moving day and she, in her childish way, was having fun unpacking them as soon as they were done, so her parents decided to have her stay with her grandparents, a six-hour drive away from her house.

Ariel remembered suddenly and very clearly having cried *in sorrow* all the way there, lying on the back seat of the car while her father drove; the child-she-was feared she was being abandoned by him and would not be allowed to come home.

What was the link with today's reality? Her father had passed away 6 months prior to this session and the sadness she felt had dredged up this event from her past "this sorrowful knot stemming from a feeling of abandonment"; this time he had left her for good. There was no relation whatsoever with the training session she had to give or even the college experience.

I then proceeded to use the inner child technique with her. While I was talking to her inner child, she felt warmth on her neck and shoulder muscles that had ached so much at the beginning of the session. She opened her eyes in disbelief to see if I was still sitting in my chair and not touching her. Through the use of tenderness, she was discovering her very own power. To self-heal. In less than 24 hours, all the pain was gone.

Together, we verified the false beliefs she had adopted and replaced them with new ones. Ariel then made the commitment to take tender care of her inner child and change her own mental programming.

John, whom I spoke about in the previous section, and who had problems at work, also came to see me for a psychokinesiology session. He felt contempt for his boss and some of his colleagues. We looked for the corresponding factor behind this feeling. This led us to the moment when he imprinted within his deepest self that he "did not have the right to exist," "did not have the right to be" thus explaining his deep contempt towards himself.

The healing of his inner child deeply affected him and taught him to give himself the consideration and the space he deserves and has every right to as a human being. He is the only one in his life now to be able to give himself recognition and fill this inner void. He is learning to manage his thoughts and emotions and take care of himself through tenderness.

> ✔ **TECHNIQUE:** Consulting

✔ CONSULTING

Now that you are aware of your situation that you have clearly identified the important issues in your life, either by writing them down or by talking to someone you can confide in, if I offered you an effective treatment that has no side effects, would you use it? Here it is: seek the help of a mental health specialist.

When you have a toothache, do you hesitate to make an appointment with the dentist? If you break an arm or a leg, do you expect it to heal by itself? Or do you choose to put it in a cast all by yourself to help it heal?

Now that your emotions are in disarray or you are bored to the point of being depressed, how long are you going to wait to heal yourself? It will cost money, you say? That is true, but would you have the same hesitation if your car engine suddenly broke down, even if the cost of repairs were through the roof? It's all a question of choices and priorities.

If seeing a health professional is no problem with respect to your physical health, why should you hesitate when it comes to your *happiness and mental health?*

This also applies to those who have read all there is to read about therapies in general and think they are self-sufficient in that regard. Unfortunately, our intellectual capabilities cannot heal our emotions; for that matter, "shoemaker's children who go barefoot!" Even therapists forget to seek help, do their inner clean-up, when it is even more essential for them to do so because of the nature of their work and the fact that it will keep them in touch with their own experience.

"COACH'S" TIP

" Be vigilant in choosing your therapist."

In recent years, a multitude of new therapies have developed in psychology, holistic medicine and personal development; this is a sign of major changes in our society which reflect an increase in the array of services being offered in response to the increase in demand.

The various approaches in psychology are becoming more and more refined; many are being modernized, and that's a good thing. Since new forms of therapy are popping up everywhere, however, you must be extra-careful when choosing a therapist and the therapy he or she practices.

It is always preferable to look for references. Call upon qualified professionals or a recognized organization before making a decision. You can never be too careful in choosing a therapy for personal development, particularly in times when you are especially vulnerable.

Take all the time you need. How long did it take you before making a decision on your last vehicle purchase? Are you not worth at least as much attention?

It is also really important that you be very comfortable with your therapist. Don't hesitate to let them know your needs and ask if they are flexible. If not, simply change therapist.

✔ **TECHNIQUE:**   Seek help from potential rescuers

☺ **Tools:**   Books on self-esteem
Training sessions

✔ SEEK HELP FROM POTENTIAL RESCUERS

There are a host of resources relating to self-esteem that are available to you. Potential rescuers may take different forms, such as a book, a community organization, or a crisis hotline.

There is a gold mine of resources to be discovered and used. Be sure of it. Do not hesitate to ask for information at your local social centers or health clinics.

☺ Books on Self-Esteem

André, Christophe & Lelord, François, *L'estime de soi : s'aimer pour mieux vivre avec les autres*, Paris, Odile Jacob, 2007.

Bradshaw, John, *Homecoming: Reclaiming and Championing Your Inner Child*, New York, Bantam Books, 1992.

Branden, Nathaniel, *The six pillars of Self-esteem*, New York, Bantam Books, 1994.

Duclos, Germain, *Quand les tout-petits apprennent à s'estimer... pour favoriser l'estime de soi des enfants de 3 à 6 ans*, CHU Sainte-Justine, 2001.

Duclos, Germain, *What Should I Know about my Child's Self-Esteem?* Montréal, Editions CHU Sainte-Justine, 2009.

Duclos, Germain, *Self-Esteem, a Passport for Life*, Montréal, CHU Sainte-Justine, 2018.

L'Écuyer, René, *Méthodologie de l'analyse développementale de contenu : Méthode GPS et concept de soi*, René, Québec, Les Presses de l'Université du Québec, 1990.

McGinnis, Alan Loy, *Bringing Out the Best in People: How to Enjoy Helping USA, Others Excel*, 2004.

Mruk, Chris, *Self-esteem: Research, Theory and Practice*, New York, Springer Publishing Company, 1995.

Newberry, Tommy, *Success is Not an Accident*, USA, 1999.

Reasoner, Robert W., *Building self-esteem*, USA, 1988.

Reasoner, Robert W. and Lane, Marylin L., *Parenting with Purpose: Five Keys to Raising Children with Values and Vision*, PersonHood Press, Ca, 2007.

Rose-Clance, Pauline Dr, *The Impostor Phenomenon: Overcoming the Fear That Haunts Your Success*, Atlanta, Peachtree Publishers,1986.

Sorensen, Marylyn J., *Breaking the chain of low Self-esteem*, Oregon, Wolf Publishing Co.,1998.

⊕ Training Sessions

As previously mentioned, a multitude of organizations offer personal development workshops of all kinds, including self-esteem. There is also an abundance of seminars and courses on parenting skills. Refer to your local health care or daycare centers, schools, and your neighbors; you will find a gold mine of information awaits you.

CHAPTER 7

MENTAL HEALTH, SELF-ESTEEM AND EPIGENETICS

~

Life's hardships can crush us and lock us in.
They can also make us stronger
and more open to others.
We didn't choose to suffer them,
yet we're free to consider them
the anvils that weigh us down,
or the foundations that lift us.

Inspired by Frédéric Lenoir

~

Mental Health

It was a real privilege for me to collaborate in Mouvement Santé Mentale Québec's five annual campaigns. This organization is dedicated to promoting mental health, and has based its materials on my theoretical model of the Five Senses of Self-Esteem.

I use their primary definition below, and have developed an informative test that will help you determine where you stand in relation to the pillars of good mental health.

A Definition of Mental Health [53]

"It is a *dynamic balance* between the various spheres of life: social, physical, spiritual, economic, emotional and mental. It allows us to act, realize our potential, face the normal difficulties in life, as well as contribute to the community. It is influenced by one's living conditions, personal values, as well as the dominant collective values."

Mental health is an essential component of overall health. It is important to specify that mental health is more than the absence of illness. In fact, "A person may live with a mental disorder, yet have good mental wellness that can be reflected in satisfying relationships or fulfilling employment."

In Reality

The WHO states that mental health problems remain one of the primary causes of absenteeism at work, loss of work and early retirement. In many developed countries, these account for 35% to 45% of all absences.

Psychological distress is caused by a network of negative emotions that, once persistent, may have serious consequences on a person's health, such as depression and anxiety.

---

53 Translated from the website of "Mouvement Santé Mentale Québec.
   https://www.mouvementsmq.ca/sante-mentale/definition

Depression is the main cause of morbidity and disability in the world; there are more than 300 million people living with this condition (WHO 2018).

Due to the aging population, by 2050, it is estimated that around 152 million people will suffer from a form of dementia, 68% of which will be from countries with middle or intermediary incomes, for an estimated of 2,000 billion dollars as of 2030.

Self-esteem is recognized as a protective factor against psychological distress. This is why prevention programs are so important and have proven their worth time and again. Furthermore, discoveries on the brain may also serve as a catalyst in increasing these trends.

⊙ Exercise: "My Mental Health"

I have matched the following pillars of mental health with the Five Senses of Self-Esteem flower. You can rate them from 1 to 10 based on your level of satisfaction.

For a more accurate self-assessment, you can reread the definitions of the senses that represent the core of self-esteem.

1 = not very satisfied, 10 = absolutely satisfied.

Afterwards, you can refer to chapter 4, "Survival Kit" to use the suggested tools and improve any of the senses in question, as needed.

So, having good mental health means	5 Senses of self-esteem	My score from 1 to 10
Being able to love life	Competency Determination	
Succeeding in putting your skills to use and reaching your goals	Competency Determination	
Establishing and maintaining relationships with others	Security Belonging	
Deriving pleasure from relationships with others	Security Belonging	
Contributing to society	Belonging Competency	
Feeling confident enough to adapt to a situation that cannot be changed, or to work towards modifying it whenever possible	Security Determination	
Developing strategies to cope with stress	Identity Security	

So, having good mental health means	5 Senses of self-esteem	My score from 1 to 10
Dealing with the inevitable difficulties of life and being able to bouncing back afterwards	Identity Determination	
Being able to ask for support from those you're close to, or from an organization specialized in helping people through difficult times	Security Belonging	
Discovering leisure activities that are enjoyable and finding time to do them	Identity Belonging	
Trying to achieve an acceptable balance between the different spheres of life: physical, psychological, economic, spiritual and social	Identity Determination	

Self-Esteem And Mental Health

Self-esteem is first and foremost a question of mental health, and can have direct repercussions on your physical health, such as neglecting your body or having psychosomatic problems. "Many psychological difficulties are linked to problems with self-esteem. They can be related to the origin of the problems (as seen with complexes), their maintenance (as seen with depression), or the shame that patients feel when confronted with social judgment (as seen with alcoholism)." [54]

Self-esteem is the primary factor in protecting self-esteem, which in turn reinforces personal resilience. We know that the positive effects of strong self-esteem contribute to good mental health in a variety of ways, such as:

Self-Esteem Contributes To	Self-esteem can treat[55]
· Stress resistance	· Anxiety
· The ability to recognize your limits	· Distress
· Resilience in overcoming obstacles	· Obsessive guilt
· Increased perseverance	· Perfectionism
· The quality of relationships	· Emotional dependence
	· Other dependencies

---

54 André, Christophe & Lelord, François (2007). *Self-Esteem, Liking Yourself in Order to Live Better With Others.*

55 Treat: providing the necessary treatment to improve an individual's health and sometimes heal them.

Furthermore, by referring to the indicators for low and healthy self-esteem previously outlined in chapter 2, it is apparent that every depressed person suffers from low self-esteem.

Balance: An Ongoing Process

I want to emphasize, that self-esteem is a continual process oscillating between your awareness of self-worth AND preserving that worth (end of Part Four). It is continual in the sense that it is lifelong.

As life changes, moves forward, and we pass through different stages, it is important to review our self-assessment in order to reinforce our self-worth. Here are some pivotal events:

· Becoming parents or grandparents. · Becoming a couple or getting divorced. · Experiencing loss.	· Completing a milestone. · Change or loss of work. · Retiring. · Emigrating.

The following statistics show that the age factor in suicide rates stands out significantly. In Québec, Canada, the number of suicides is higher among men and women aged 50 to 64 years.

In France, people aged 45 to 54 years, and those over 75, are shown to be the most at-risk populations with excessive suicide mortality rates of 25.1 and 30 per 100,000 inhabitants. Taking into account the entire population, the suicide mortality rate is 16.7 per 100,000 inhabitants. According to the World Health Organization, suicide is the second-highest cause of death, after traffic accidents, for people aged 15 to 23 years.

Balance: The Foundation of Good Mental Health

Self-esteem can also be defined as the perception of self-worth that we recognize in the different spheres of our life! It is the opinion that we have of each of our "selves" across these dimensions.

What is your opinion of *your self-worth* in the physical, mental, social, financial and spiritual dimensions? It would be interesting to review your "GPS / Personal Self-Esteem Balance Sheet" in Exercise 3 (Your Self-Esteem per Life Sphere).

In order to maintain good mental health, it is important to achieve balance between the different spheres of life… Otherwise, you could end up having a breakdown.

Once, my psychologist suggested that a 24-hour day should be divided between 8 hours of work, 8 hours of sleep, and 8 hours for personal and social hygiene: I literally almost choked! I was working around 90 hours a week. Without a minute to myself: a single parent with sole custody of my children, a self-employed worker, a volunteer at an alternative school, with serious financial stress… I only existed within my roles, stuck in survival mode.

Balance: not only a foreign word to me at the time, but one that I thought was impossible to apply to myself in those days… That is, right up until the moment that burnout caught up with me, and I had to learn how to balance my activities more effectively.

Feelings: Receiving Messages

The feelings or physical tensions that we feel are actually messages that our body is transmitting to us. They act as an alarm signal. Their purpose is to bring us back into contact with our inner self, our fundamental core.

Some people experience physical discomfort: migraines, insomnia, etc. Others experience a kind of uneasiness inside, they feel uncomfortable … like wearing a piece of clothing that is the wrong size, too small or too large. Sometimes they become anxious or distressed. These are our warning signs! Our own built-in indicators!

Now is the ideal time to evaluate your situation and remind yourself that the beliefs you hold about life and about yourself are the ones that guide you.

The 21st Century: The Fabulous Discoveries on the Brain

Numerous discoveries in neuroscience have confirmed our own power as an individual over our personal development, both biologically and mentally, and the relationship between them. Here is where mind-body medicine comes in.

Brain Plasticity

The growth of neuroscience[56], due to the advent of MRIs, has paved the way to deciphering thoughts, emotions, motivations, etc. This vital contribution has uncovered one of the most promising discoveries to date: the brain's properties of "plasticity."

Plasticity represents the capacity for the brain to create and modify its connections in order to adapt to the organism's internal changes, the environment, and even the individual's experiences with respect to habits or behaviors.

For example, when we learn something new or rise to a challenge, the neural network in our cortex transforms. We have the biological ability to modify our brain and adopt healthier attitudes. Science has proven that nothing is ever permanently fixed in our brain because "the brain is trainable and deformable"!

Epigenetics

Until recently, science explained that we were programmed by our genetic inheritance. Then came the epigenetics revolution!

Within a few years, this revolution had shaken up the biology world by proving that "*the environment* where we evolve, *the food* that we consume, *the behaviors and beliefs* that we adopt, and *the personal and social relationships* that we cultivate are factors that modulate, activate or block the activity of our genes. In other words, the 'dictatorship' of genes does not exist[57]" for we truly have power over them.

Recent studies have shown that our way of life, both physically and emotionally, has a real effect on our DNA and may or may not trigger the genes linked to familial illnesses. Also, our lifestyles, our food, and our history equally influence the biological legacy that we pass on.

This means we are able to reprogram our genes, improve our life as well as the life of our descendants! PHEW! What a marvelous discovery! And all by acting upon our environment and adopting better hygiene in all spheres of life, and even love. Please read what comes next.

---

56 Towards a Neuro-Society: can everything be explained through cerebral imaging?
   https://theconversation.com/vers-une-neuro-societe-tout-peut-il-sexpliquer-par-limagerie-cerebrale-94346
57 Urman, Valérie (2018), *La Révolution épigénétique (The Epigenetic Revolution)*.

The Power of Love Over DNA[58]

Here is a concrete example: this study showed that the love we receive produces an effect on our DNA, and the love we give can prevent the transmission of trauma to our children. "Love acts upon the very heart of our genome, to cleanse our whole being from past pain." What fascinating times!

Our Body and Depression

A psychiatrist in California, Dr. Daniel Amen, proposed a theoretical model of care based on the following premise: "A mental illness is almost always related to an anatomical anomaly in the brain through various factors, such as a shock, intoxication or dysfunctions." As a pioneer in brain imaging, he laments that psychiatrists are the only specialists that never see the organ they treat.

In his approach, the brain is an organ that can evolve and can be restored by eliminating the causes of illness (inflammation, allergies, and others) and providing it with essential elements (food, oxygen, supplemental Gaba, etc.)... and occasionally, medication.

Other discoveries in neuropsychiatry have established the link between inflammatory conditions (infection or chronic diseases) and type 2 diabetes: these symptoms affect the brain by lowering neurotransmitters such as serotonin, which can trigger the onset of depression.

In my early forties, I was having symptoms of depression and I went to see my doctor. After his opening question of "How are you?" I burst into tears. A quick diagnosis of depression and prescription for antidepressants followed. I still asked to go for blood tests and decided to wait on the results before starting my new prescription. I ended up having a positive test result for hypothyroidism, which was a game changer ... and of course, I was given another prescription.

Six months later, I returned to the clinic and explained that I was feeling better, but still not 100% in shape in terms of energy. His new prescription was: "We're in June now, the sun will surely do you some good". Outraged, I left his office and found myself another doctor who applied a more, shall we say, comprehensive approach.

Why share this anecdote with you? Because we should not follow everything to the letter and BELIEVE everything that is said to us, even by a medical authority.

58 Study by Moshe Szyf and Michael Meaney on maternal care effect (2004): Epigenetic Programming by Maternal behavior. As we mentioned in chapter 5.

The Biology of Belief and Its Effects[59]

From the moment I came across this book, its title both challenged and intrigued me. Written by a doctor of molecular biology and quantum physics, it is quite compelling in that it eloquently reveals the effects of our beliefs on our biology.

Dr. Lipton discusses the "Belief Effect," rather than the placebo effect, highlighting that our perceptions, both correct and incorrect, work in the same way on our behavior and our body. This means that the mind and body have an incredible capacity to heal themselves, and the fact of using this energy has no side effects compared to medications.

In *"You are the Placebo"* [60] the author demonstrates that patients with major dysfunctions such as crippling arthritis, heart disease and even Parkinson's tremors have managed to reverse their symptoms simply by believing in the power of a placebo, without any side effects. On the other hand, "nocebos[61]" have influenced certain people who fell ill and even died, having been mistakenly diagnosed with a fatal disease. "Our beliefs are more powerful than reality!"

HOW LONG will it take for scientific research on the placebo effect to advance? It may be postponed indefinitely, since it would negatively affect the pharmaceutical industry, which is known to delete data when the placebo is shown to be as effective as the medication.

One university study out of California[62] confirmed that we can estimate the ability to be happy, 50% of which depends on genetic determinants, 10% is linked to lifestyle and external factors, and the remaining 40% stem from our own personal efforts.

FASCINATING! Science has proven that using our genes as an excuse is no longer valid! Our inherent powers over our emotions, our mood and our beliefs are official and confirm more than ever that we are fully responsible for our own happiness.

---

59 Lipton, Bruce (2015). *The Biology of Belief: Unleashing the Power of Consciousness, Matter & Miracles.*

60 Dispenza, Joe (2015). *You Are the Placebo: Making Your Mind Matter.*

61 The Nocebo Effect is produced by negative expectations in relation to a treatment, a product or a prediction.

62 Lenoir, Frédéric (2015). *Happiness. A Philosopher's Guide.*

The Brain Is Fabulous... And Is Still Uncharted Territory!

What Buddha said more than 2500 years ago has now been proven by science!

What you think, you become

What you feel, you attract

What you imagine, you create

Buddha

Over many years, I have stated that: "We repair hearts in cardiology and even perform miracles, while in psychology, we remain in the era of Freud's couch: unthinkable and unacceptable!" The law of attraction is what first drew me to psychokinesiology[63]. I practiced its muscle testing (as reliable as a laser), and then tried Dr. Bach's Original Flower Remedies, a treatment whose speed and effectiveness was fast with a capital F. That which you seek, you will find! AND YES! It is possible to heal psychologically, both quickly and completely, in this 21st century!

Body / Mind Techniques

Body / mind techniques contribute to quality of life and overall health, and should be complemented by traditional care. *Integrative medicine (IM)*[64] considers the client as a whole (body, mind, environment). This approach combines conventional medicine AND different forms of alternative therapies. Many universities are currently reviewing their teaching curriculum in medicine in order to integrate complementary approaches whose benefits have already been proven. It is still interesting to see how the current situation is limited by the established order that have been putting on the brakes... I can attest to that, having been followed as a patient in IM to this day.

Science is amazing! But in practice? Here is a brief summary of the proven effects of gratitude and meditation, techniques that are user-friendly.

---

63 A technique based on kinesiology, Chinese medicine, acupuncture and psychotherapy. See chapter 6.

64 Integrative medicine is keeping up with scientific developments, it includes all therapeutic approaches and appropriate specializations to achieve optimal health.

The Effects of Gratitude[65]

Numerous studies in positive psychology have shown that gratitude has beneficial effects on the hopelessness of suicidal patients, on depression, addiction, human relations, sleep, physical health and happiness, including increasing longevity by more than seven years.

The Effects of Meditation

One particular study using brain imaging found the propensity of neurons to create connections in people who have trained in meditation, such as the Tibetan monk Mathieu Ricard. The practice of full consciousness positively impacts our state of health. As Dr. Deepak Chopra says: "Regular meditation develops awareness of an ageless body and a timeless mind."

With respect to cardiac coherence, there is abundant proof of its ability to calm anxiety, improve sleep, adrenal function and brain plasticity, which in turn improves decision-making skills.

Avant-garde Tools

Here are some additional techniques that I have personally tested, and which gave me excellent results in improving my mental health.

- Self-hypnosis in alpha state: helps to better deal with our emotional states and stress, increase intuition and achieve exceptional programming results.

- Brain Gym®: to balance and coordinate the brain, vision, hearing, writing and movement, in order to facilitate communication, centering, comprehension and concentration.

- The muscle testing of kinesiology used to access cellular memory, like a laser beam.

- Dr. Bach's Original Flower Remedies: 38 flower essences to balance 38 emotions.

Brain and Self-Esteem

Scientists have confirmed that we use only 5 to 10 percent of our brain. What is the vast potential of the remaining 95 percent?

Now that the relationship between body / brain / mind has been clearly established, we can certainly extrapolate the domino effect on self-esteem, seeing as the latter represents our thoughts and perceptions. When will the self-esteem neuron be discovered?

---

65 Angelard, Christine (2018). *La gratitude qui guérit. Comment soigner les blessures du passé (Gratitude That Heals. How to Treat the Wounds of the Past).*

"Science gathers knowledge faster than society gathers wisdom." (Isaac Asimov). My wish? That everyone has the wisdom to take responsibility and commit to their health by researching the new possibilities in mental health care.

In sum, the practices that act on the brain: psychotherapy, meditation, gratitude, mental programming, diet, etc., have positive effects and are indisputable everyday allies in preserving our mental health and self-esteem.

~

Reprogramming
for our mental health and self-esteem
and aging serenely!

~

CHAPTER 8

REPROGRAMMING BELIEFS LINKED TO SELF-ESTEEM

~

Nothing binds you, except your thoughts.

Nothing limits you, except your fears.

And nothing controls you, except your beliefs.

Marianne Williamson

~

Reprogramming Beliefs Linked to Self-Esteem

What is a Belief?

"A belief is not only an idea that the mind possesses; it is an idea that possesses the mind"; I love this quote which expresses the essence, the blind force of belief that propels our behavior.

In fact, if we understand as the law of attraction attests, that our thoughts work magnetically, attracting what we believe, then taking responsibility for our own happiness and fulfillment becomes more apparent than ever.

The Link Between Beliefs and Self-Esteem

The primary definition of self-esteem, *the awareness of our self-worth*, states that self-esteem is based on the beliefs that we hold about ourselves. Misguided beliefs will produce low self-esteem and vice versa.

A belief is an idea that we "believe" to be true. To improve our self-esteem, we must rely on the accuracy of our convictions, which often need to be realigned or reprogrammed.

It is true; these beliefs are imprinted on everything that we feel, including the value we place on ourselves, essentially working like a thermostat that regulates the degree of our accomplishments, successes and failures. In fact, neither willpower nor determination can compete with the power of our ingrained beliefs.

Likewise, our accomplishments, successes and failures work in some respects like a thermometer or mirror, reflecting the degree or quality of our convictions which can determine to what extent these conclusions about ourselves and about life will be positive or negative.

Types of Beliefs: Conscious and Unconscious

Our personal history allows us to register EVERYTHING that we have experienced from the moment of conception to now, and this experience is etched in each of our cells. This is what is called cellular memory.

There are a large number of conscious beliefs that can be easily identified by the content of our spoken or written words. However, unconscious beliefs leave deep "engrams[66]" in our body and our psyche, and require more specific techniques to detect them. The kinesiology muscle test has proven to be a powerful tool in this regard.

The Source of Our Beliefs

Many other psychological threads make up the fabric of our belief system. This mental architecture is built from the accumulation of many beliefs of various origins such as *personal, familial, national and ancestral.*

Like a Computer

In order to clarify the importance and impact of our beliefs, I will make a comparison between our psyche and a computer.

3 Levels	Include	Similar to
CONSCIOUS	Thoughts, ideas, reflections, speech	COMPUTER
SUBCONSCIOUS	Beliefs, personal and familial programming	SOFTWARE / PROGRAMS
UNCONSCIOUS	Personal Unconscious	OPERATING SYSTEM
	Collective Unconscious: "the memory of everything" including national and ancestral beliefs, and symbolization	HARD DISK / INTERNET

---

66 The engrams are biological traces of memory.

Here are some examples of beliefs you may have heard and possibly integrated:

YOU WERE TOLD: "You..." (Message heard and received)	YOU BELIEVE: "I am..." (Message understood, accepted and transformed into an engram)
You cannot make a living from your passion; you will starve to death.	*I cannot make a living from my passion.*
You do not have enough talent (or potential) to succeed.	*I do not have enough talent or potential to succeed.*
You are stubborn...	*I am stubborn.*
You are an idiot...	*I am an idiot.*
We are unlucky (because we are poor, uneducated...)	*I am unlucky, I come from a (poor, uneducated, etc.) environment.*
We, as Americans, are not ... lucky, spoiled...	*I am not... lucky, spoiled.*

Genetic Baggage and History [67]

While it is true that we construct our beliefs on a daily basis, we need an additional intellectual exercise to understand the unconscious accumulation of a multitude of other beliefs, spoken and unspoken, which come from our family or social environment.

For example, we have often heard the expression "born on the wrong side of the tracks," a reductive assertion whose negative connotation undermines people's potential for success. There is an equivalent French expression, used in Québec, which I was able to validate on numerous occasions, through muscular testing. I discovered that many youths had integrated this belief *even if they had never heard tell of it* in their family.

Every one of us has a family heritage etched into our psyche and DNA, which carries our genetic and well as historical baggage. For example, during one consultation, a client with[68] bulimia was able to correct her behavior after realizing her beliefs were linked to ancestors who had died of starvation. Many others have been able to retrace beliefs that were anchored in the psyche of

---

67 Schutzenberger, Ancelin (1998). *The Ancestor Syndrome: Transgenerational Psychotherapy and the Hidden Links in the Family.*

68 For more details on this case, refer to my French book (2003): *La tendresse: chemin de guérison des émotions et du corps par la psychokinésiologie, la science de la tendresse*, p.72.

their family line for generations. Remember, traumas can be imprinted on the genes for three generations.

Our past, whether recent or remote, can alter our beliefs and while we may wish to honor it, we are responsible for moving towards a better future. This is why reprogramming our assertions is crucial and allows us to "let go" of these totally unconscious beliefs.

> *The past is a place of reference and not a place of residence!*
> **Martin Latulippe**

Why Reprogram Our Beliefs?

Your level of happiness and success has nothing to do with what is potentially available to you (or not), it is determined by your beliefs. Remember that your life is a reflection of what you have inside.

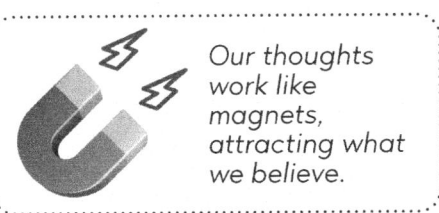

Our thoughts work like magnets, attracting what we believe.

At the end of the day, it is always about acknowledging, in all humility, that we have fully participated in creating what happens to us by the very nature of our thoughts and beliefs.

⊘ How to Change Our Beliefs

Refer to chapter 6: Personalized First-Aid Kit, and the section "Controlling My Thoughts / Mental Programming" to remind yourself of what it takes to change your beliefs, and the importance of doing so, just like updating a computer.

Here are three steps that will guide you through the process of changing your beliefs.

1. Identify Them

Clearly identifying your beliefs is really important. You already recognize a number of beliefs that limit you. For others, the muscle test in kinesiology will confirm them in a few seconds[69].

2. Eliminate Them

Steadfast proponents of positive thinking have overlooked this step; however, it is essential to eliminate the incessant refrain of negative beliefs before they can be replaced.

---

69 Frost, Robert (2013). *Applied Kinesiology, A Training Manual and Reference Book of Basic Principles and Practices*, Chap.3.

This symbolic method consists of writing down the false belief, crossing it out with a large red X, ripping it to shreds, throwing it out, and writing down a new, positive affirmation.

3. Reprogram Them

Now, write down the new belief that you wish to adopt. Use "I" and the present tense in the affirmative, as if it is a quality that you already have.

> *Positive thinking, by itself, cannot erode false beliefs.*

Then, let it cure for a minimum of 21 days; it takes multiple repetitions a day to replace your malicious software... Reprogramming is accomplished by:

- **Repeating** the new affirmation: silently, out loud, in song, in your head.

- **Visualizing your new, positive affirmations.**

- Ideally, for optimal results, you should focus and visualize or rehearse them as pictures, while in **alpha mode**.

Does Reprogramming Our Beliefs Really Work?

IT IS ABSOLUTELY CERTAIN that affirmations can modify our beliefs. In my experience, as well as my thirty years of professional practice, I can say that it is true in 95% of cases, under certain conditions.

These winning conditions contribute to convincing results:

- Keep it *consistent*: You should avoid undermining the affirmations between repetitions by thinking or saying the opposite; otherwise, it cancels the magnetic effect.

- *Keep on believing*: Cease all inner doubt. Have confidence in the process. You are not lying to yourself … you are stating the truth in advance!

The remaining 5% are inconclusive:

Certain beliefs will be hard to eradicate IF they come from deep-seated hurt or trauma. It is worthwhile investigating further to find out the origin of the false belief that produced the engram.

At the beginning of my working life, I joined a multi-level marketing company because I had this dream of one day creating a school.

For more than 15 years, I put my dream on hold to develop this new business in which I passionately invested myself, mind and body. However, despite diligently applying these effective programming techniques, I was not able to achieve certain goals that I had set my heart on. Some people thought that I had made enviable progress, but honestly, I felt my star was still beyond my reach.

In hindsight, I understood why it had never worked for me before: I had terrible self-esteem! In keeping with my family and inherited beliefs, I had been unable to 'see' myself succeed and reach the summit. I had to work on my self-esteem for many years afterwards in order to get to a place where I felt I had a right to succeed, without working myself to death in the process.

Affirmations Linked to Self-Esteem

Where my Lexicon of Self-Affirmation Comes From

What follows is a compilation of twenty years of practice in counseling individuals in psychokinesiology. From hundreds of clients' files, I have identified these self-esteem affirmations and classified them, along with their components from the Five Senses of Self-Esteem Flower, into a complete lexicon from A (Acceptance) to Z (Zenitude).

Gender

Out of respect for the clients and our therapeutic relationship, I wanted to keep the same gender (female and male) of the real-life affirmation that was created during the original consultation. Please do not be offended, simply modify the affirmation as you wish.

How to Use the Lexicon

Based on your *GPS / Personal Self-Esteem Balance Sheet* (chapter 3) and your current needs, look through the lexicon for the affirmations that you wish to apply; use them word-for-word or in combination with others.

Considering the decisive scope of unconscious intergenerational beliefs, it's best to try to eliminate them. This is why, at the end of some of the categories, I have included the affirmation "Let it go" in reference to those beliefs that are rooted in family or ancestral heritage. Use them preventatively. You'll be astonished at the effect on your psyche!

Lexicon from A to Z

Acceptance

I accept all my power as a woman.

I am learning to know, accept and love myself, more and more.

I accept myself 100%: as I am, with all of my imperfections, strengths, and limitations.

I accept myself in my humanity, and therefore, I accept others as they are, where they are.

I accept myself more and more every day.

I accept myself: imperfect, free, happy and proud to be me!

I accept myself as I am because I am a man: I am worth my weight in gold.

I accept myself as I am: in body, identity and name.

I let go of all the limiting personal, family and inherited beliefs related to fully accepting who I am.

Belonging (see Place)

I enjoy the freedom to express myself with my own family.

I am beginning a new cycle of self-confidence and security for my descendants.

I feel valued to be a part of this group.

I respect my needs and I am prepared to leave … (group or business).

I am well integrated in my milieu / my family.

I am committed and reliable in my relationships.

I am proud of my family / or to carry my family name.

I am free to be a part of … (a group close to you).

It's great to be part of this clan!

Comparison

I have as much value as anyone else (or name someone).

I love myself unconditionally, independent of others' gaze.

I am awesome and extraordinary! I have nothing to prove to anyone: I follow my own path!

I am truly aligned with my destiny, and I deserve it as much as anyone else.

I am unique and magnificent and I have the right to shine as much as anyone.

I am as worthy as men are.

When I compare myself, I realize how wonderful I am, and I rejoice for who I am.

If I compare myself, I acknowledge my full worth, with all my skills and potential.

Competency (see Talents)

I agree to use all of my skills to the best of my ability, and be proud of them.

I have the necessary talent, ability and potential to achieve all of my dreams.

I recognize all my strengths and talents and I bring them to fruition through actions that serve others.

I assert myself in all facets of my personality: It's better to be whole than to be perfect.

I am at the top of my game, I go with the flow and I am in full possession of my physical and psychological abilities.

I am conscious of my abilities, and I actively exploit them.

I am extraordinary, and I have full confidence in my potential to succeed.

My professional life is fulfilling and encompasses all of my business acumen and artistic talents.

I let go of all the limiting personal, family and inherited beliefs related to my abilities and my right to be successful.

Determination

I take responsibility for my choices, and I will forever risk making mistakes.

I am proud of setting yearly goals and doing everything I can to achieve them.

I accept who I am and wield full power over my own life.

I have all the courage it takes to deal with whatever happens in my life.

I have every means at my disposal to manage my attitudes and achieve my goals.

I am able to maintain a balanced lifestyle in order to succeed in my life and life in general.

I am more and more determined to carry out my plans.

I am fully aware of my aptitudes and can boldly and happily handle anything that comes my way.

I am resilient and I have found my way!

Dignity

I clearly deserve to be treated with dignity!

I humbly accept to ask for or receive help when I need it.

I am allowed to make mistakes and am able to tenderly apologize for them.

I celebrate myself fully as a unique individual and act as such with my partner.

I focus on the "good" in me.

I can choose to be single in order to live a balanced lifestyle.

I respect my values by ensuring that my partner respects them as well.

My life is worth living: I own it!

When I say no to someone, I am saying yes to myself.

I let go of all the limiting personal, family and inherited beliefs related to my self-worth and my right to dignity, pure and simple!

Identity

I like and am happy with my true nature: sensitive, idealistic, and intellectual.

I am beautiful, inside and out.

I am aware of my intuition, my resources, and my innate qualities: I take a bite out of life!

I am a radiant, brilliant being who enjoys a balanced life.

I am a unique, original, creative and wonderful being.

I am 100% a man, exuding confidence and charisma.

Because I am a woman / man: I am worth my weight in gold.

Tah dah! I am myself, the real me, and proud of it!

I let go of all the limiting personal, family and inherited beliefs related to my unique, original and creative nature.

Kindness (see Regard)

I accept myself with kindness.

I embrace myself and am loyal to myself more and more every day.

I love myself enough to prioritize and take care of myself properly.

I take precious care of my needs, my health and my aspirations.

I gladly take care of myself, with the assurance that I am the number one priority in my own life.

I take care of myself as a woman, which pleases me and allows me to grow.

I take care of myself: I rest and stop when I want to and when I feel the need. Every day, I am kinder and gentler with myself.

My place

I can take my place in all my relationships and leave room for others.

There is a big, beautiful place for me in the sun!

I agree to fully occupy my space and honor my talents and dreams.

I choose to live and to fully and peacefully take my place in the Universe by divine right.

I deserve my "VIP" status, and I take full advantage of it.

I am present within myself first, rather than taking up space with my body.

I am at a healthy weight because I respect the limits of my physical and spiritual space.

Daring to take my place will create a joyous surge of wellbeing because everyone is free to react in their own way.

Fulfilling my soul's mandate erases all my limiting personal, family and inherited beliefs related to professional success and the place of women.

My rights

I have the right to my vital space, and I occupy it fully.

I have the right to be myself, fully and entirely, with my strengths and weaknesses, allowing me to live authentically and joyfully.

I have the right to live fully and completely.

I have the right to say no, which means saying, "yes" to myself.

I have the right to act silly.

I carry my VIP card with me, which gives me access to all the benefits and success to which I aspire.

I make my presence known using my mind, humor and creativity in an appropriate manner.

I am a magnificent sun who has the right to shine in the directions I choose.

I let go of all the limiting personal, family and inherited beliefs related to my right to exist.

Security

I trust in life's process and I feel secure.

I can safely say what I think and assert my needs.

I can safely be who I am, personally, professionally and spiritually so that I can accomplish my mission in life.

I am in full control of my life; I take care of my own security.

I feel secure in the Universe.

I feel safe in a plane (train, car, on the road).

I feel safe and protected in the presence of my invisible spiritual Guides who are by my side at all times.

My daughter receives guidance and is safe and protected.

I let go of all the limiting personal, family and inherited beliefs related to attachment, presence and security.

Self-affirmation

At work and in my projects, I can easily assert myself with clarity and conviction.

It's "cool" to act gently but firmly.

I don't care what others think of me.

Speaking up just means presenting my point of view alongside others' in order to find a solution.

I assert myself with sensitivity and conviction in order to enjoy meaningful, harmonious relationships.

I am totally myself, and I assert myself fully.

I hold my own (point of view), reasonably and fairly, and I stand tall!

Asserting myself means ensuring that I get more out of life and my relationships with others.

Love me or Leave Me!

I let go of all the limiting personal, family and inherited beliefs related to self-affirmation, abundance and success.

Self-confidence

I have more and more confidence in myself and my decisions.

I radiate confidence and self-respect.

I believe in my creative potential more and more and I nurture it in active and tangible ways.

I truly believe in my potential and myself.

I allow men and women that respect me to approach me in complete confidence.

I believe in myself because I am fully grounded.

I am extraordinary and I feel better and better in my own skin.

I am a treasure that I am willing to show others.

Self-love

I love myself 100% as I am, without waiting to be perfect.

I love myself as much as I love my best friend (add a name here).

I love myself more and more, and I approve of myself.

I love and have a good opinion of myself.

I love myself enough to attract a balanced romantic relationship.

I am filled with peace and security thanks to my self-love.

My self-love depends on me, and me alone, and it fulfills me completely.

The best gift I can give myself is to love myself unconditionally.

I let go of all the limiting personal, family and inherited beliefs related to how others view me and love me.

Self-recognition (see Identity)

You have to know yourself before you can recognize yourself. G.D.

I appreciate my talents and strengths and I am proud of myself.

I get to know myself and appreciate the treasure that I am (qualities, talents and more).

I am proud to be me, the real (your name) for all to see.

I recognize my great worth.

I naturally and fully recognize the beauty and good in me.

I fully recognize my talents, skills and creativity, which I celebrate: Hurray!

I am the architect of my own life, and therefore, I am important.

I am unique, magnificent, and proud of it!

I let go of all the limiting personal, family and inherited beliefs related to self-recognition.

Self-regard (see Kindness)

Every time I look into my own eyes (do this in front of the mirror), I lovingly remind myself of who I am and of my mission in life.

I exist firstly in how I perceive myself and I truly appreciate what I see.

I see myself and recognize my true worth: a real treasure.

I consider myself as a man, with honesty and kindness.

I am deeply convinced of my self-worth, with or without the approval of others.

My own opinion of myself is worth more than others'.

The men in my life fully accept and embrace who I am, and they treat me with consideration.

In perceiving myself, I simply recognize the value in what I am, what I say, what I do and what I possess.

I let go of all the limiting personal, family and inherited beliefs related to my father and mother's view of my successes.

Sensitivity

I accept my sensitivity as a gift, an advantage.

I accept that I am a sensitive and fragile person and I show my vulnerability.

I recognize my sensitivity as an advantage, and I learn to channel it in positive ways.

I'm so proud to be "a sensitive soul."

My deep sensitivity is a gift from the gods; I take care of it because it allows me to listen to others and stay connected to my Source.

Crying just means expressing my sensitive heart.

I let go of all the limiting personal, family and inherited beliefs related to my sensitivity and uniqueness.

Success (see Competency, Talents)

I now have everything I need to easily succeed.

I express all of my potential and I savor my success: Yeah!

I radiate success from every pore.

I deserve to be successful and I succeed in everything I undertake.

I am confident in my success by divine right.

I believe in my success: a (family name) can succeed with flying colors.

I am in the driver's seat: I believe in myself and in my ability to build a fabulous future.

My current success consists in being satisfied at all times and radiating happiness.

I let go of all the limiting personal, family and inherited beliefs related to my right to unlimited success.

Talents (see Competency)

I agree to shine with my unique qualities and talents.

I exploit my potential in every sphere of my life and I seamlessly combine my rational side with my talents and gifts.

I joyfully use my talents to serve others and humanity.

I am overflowing with talents and have resources to last a lifetime.

I feel profound joy when sharing my artistic talents: It's my life's mission.

I am open to the idea of monetizing my talents and then the phone rings!

My ideal scenario is to be able to nurture my creative talent.

My innovative and creative leadership is highly appreciated and constantly in demand.

I let go of all the limiting personal, family and inherited beliefs related to my gifts and talents.

Trust in life and in others (see Security)

Life is so beautiful and it just keeps going non-stop: It's fantastic!

I trust in myself and in life, and it pays me back tenfold.

I am learning to trust the girls that I spend time with, and I am now just as comfortable with them as I am with boys.

I trust in life for the future of my children.

I have trust in *my* life; it knows the best and easiest direction for me to take.

I have blind faith in life, an ally I can always rely on for opportunities that are worthwhile and beneficial.

Everything that I need comes to me at the ideal place and time.

I trust that everything I believe in, and waiting for, will happen in my life: I have the right to shoot for the moon!

I let go of all the limiting personal, family and inherited beliefs related to confidence and success.

Worth (see Self-Regard)

I am worth as much as a man and I deserve the same respect, attention and place.

I am so worthy that I deserve to take care of myself and follow my dreams and aspirations to the end.

I believe in my self-worth and my ability as a (insert your trade or profession: writer, teacher, etc.).

I deserve to love, be loved and be paid what I am worth: I'm worth a lot!

I recognize my skills and talents for what they are worth; therefore, I deserve to succeed in every sphere of my life.

I am proud of my life's path and the lessons I have learned that enable me to believe in love and in my self-worth.

I am worth my weight in gold! I am proud of myself!

My intrinsic value is immeasurable.

I let go of all the limiting personal, family and inherited beliefs related to my self-worth and any form of comparison.

Zenitude

My strength lies in being calm and confident!

I am here and now!

I am allowed to relax and even do nothing, peacefully and happily.

I feel centered, relaxed and more and more secure.

I feel more and more Zen.

Life is wonderful and I am very happy to live in the joy of the present moment.

Life is simple and gets easier all the time.

"Peace, know I am here!" [70]

---

70 From my ebook "Remember who you are." (2014).

CHAPTER 9

AND NOW
TO CONCLUDE...

We either make ourselves miserable,
or we make ourselves strong.
The amount of work is the same.

Don Juan

Epilogue:
My Survival Through
Self-Esteem!

This guide was meant as a passport to good health. I like to borrow from the Quebec psychoanalyst and reputable author, Guy Corneau's definition of health which goes beyond 'the absence of illness': 'Being healthy means loving yourself as you are, in all of life's successive moments… It's loving yourself with your flaws, your lack of love for yourself and others, your refusal to be open, your pleasure in doing so.' [71] It's accepting to be yourself!

Throughout this guide, I've shared with you the road I've traveled: the dramatic moments, the tools that I learned and applied to overcome obstacles. To remain honest with you, I also want you to know the happy outcomes that having better self-esteem helped me to achieve.

On the romantic side of things, I took the necessary time to change my beliefs and convince myself that I deserved to be loved for myself. I attracted my soul mate, and together we built a promising and serene future. We live in the very essence of the relationship that I had programmed, with "communication, harmony and tenderness." The depth of our feelings along with our spiritual beliefs allowed us to sanctify our profound happiness. Everyone deserves this oasis of peace and love. So do you!

My life goals became easier and easier to reach because they were truly mine, molded to my own aspirations and not coming from outside pressures. If it so happens that they are taking time to achieve, I verify the beliefs that could be hindering me, and then figure out if I have to change direction.

---

71 Corneau, Guy (2000). *La guérison du cœur (Healing the Heart).*

In terms of my friendships and other social relationships, I was able to assert myself successfully by taking into account my needs and taking care of myself above all. No one was going to do it for me. I no longer keep relationships on principle alone, but choose to do so only if I am sure they fulfill me. I realize that my relationships with others now reflect the relationship that I have with myself.

Professionally, I have essentially gotten rid of any doubts I had about my abilities. I am now aware of my power to create the present and the future. My life is filled with satisfaction, accomplishments and harmony. I now believe that I deserve to succeed. I let go of all useless safeguards: I trust in life. And life gives back in kind!

I am convinced that "what is best for me will come at the right time." I believe that all the events that I have lived through in my life have brought me to the state of awareness that I enjoy today, and that all the hurt I experienced made me open to my spiritual self and my mission.

This is what my odyssey looked like, the journey toward self-esteem by which I was able to survive; some will find it a bumpy and difficult ride: Such was mine. Perhaps you were lucky enough to have followed a more direct path, without as many pitfalls, so much the better. The goal is to get to your destination, the place where you made an appointment with your wonderful self! You have all the powers it takes!

Reminders to Live By

Here is a summary of the main ideas that underlie the philosophy of "Survival through Self-esteem."

1. Stay in touch with yourself: your tastes, limits and the ebb and flow of your energy. Relearn yourself as needed. Discovering the individuality within yourself, the unique, and distinct being that you are, will help you achieve a sense of inner security. This requires some willpower and training on your part. Happiness comes from within.

2. Regardless of what it is, your past does not define you. Realize the things that happen in your life are there to remind you of past hurts, and give you the chance to heal. Particularly true for those who have children.

3. Don't feel bad: No one is perfect!
   "The idea ... is that perfection belongs to the gods and completeness is the greatest thing a human being can aspire to," which is why Jung said: "It's better to be whole than to be perfect."

   Accept yourself as you are and repeat: "*I am what I am and I cannot avoid the light of my personality, nor its shadow!*" Your life is a work of art, and you are the artist.

4. Thanks to the brain's plasticity, it can be rewired: learning new things can change the connections in the brain. You have the power to influence your biology and your DNA by the way you live, both physically and emotionally, and by your mental programming.

5. Keep an open mind when it comes to innovative, tremendous avenues, such as in integrative medicine, that will appear in the future in regards to mental health. This will require the wisdom to take charge of and commit to your health.

6. Finally ... don't count on your memory; as a precaution, keep this "survival guide" close at hand in case of emergency, as you would a life preserver on a boat. It may very well be useful during those times when your self-esteem is fluctuating.

Afterwards...?
The First Step

You can keep all of these tools with you on your life's journey. But where to begin?

THERE IS ONLY ONE WAY FORWARD, AND THAT IS THROUGH TENDERNESS!

Be good to yourself, be kind! Transform your small successes into great victories and your mistakes into minor issues that are unimportant. Learn to celebrate yourself, even when it's not your birthday!

LOVE YOURSELF! It's the KEY TO YOUR HEALTH! No one can give you what you can't provide for yourself, and for that matter, it's the best example you can give your children. BE YOUR BEST SELF!

There comes a time in life
when you have no
other choice
but to make your own way.

A time to follow your dreams.

A time to hoist the sails of your own beliefs." [72]

Your time is now!

Enjoy using your inherent powers over your happiness and self-worth!

---

72 Bambaren, Sergio (1995). *The Dolphin: Story of a Dreamer.*

Bibliography

You will also find a list of books on self-esteem in chapter 6.

Angelard, Christine, *La gratitude qui guérit. Comment soigner les blessures du passé*, Montréal, Édito, 2018.

Bambaren, Sergio, *The Dolphin: Story of a Dreamer*, Australia, McPhersons Group, 1995. (In Spanish: El delfín, Fuera de coleccion, Mass Market, 2004.)

Braverman, Eric, *The Edge Effect*, New York, Sterling Publishing, 2005.

Cyrulnik, Boris, *The Whispering of Ghosts: Trauma and Resilience*, New York, Other Press, 2010.

Corneau, Guy, *La Guérison du cœur*, Montréal, Éditions de l'Homme, 2000.

Dispenza, Joe, *You Are the Placebo: Making Your Mind Matter*, USA, 2015.

Lenoir, Frédéric, *Happiness. A Philosopher's Guide*, New York, Melville House, 2016.

Lévesque, Aline et Flückiger, Hedwidge, *La Tendresse: chemin de guérison des émotions et du corps par la psycho-kinésiologie, science de la tendresse*, Brossard, Éditions Un monde différent, 2003.

Lipton, Bruce, *The Biology of Belief: Unleashing the Power of Consciousness*, 10th Anniversary Edition, Matter & Miracles, USA, Hay House, 2016.

Miller, Alice, *The Drama of the Gifted Child, The Search for the True Self*, New York, 3rd edition, Basic Books, 2007.

Miller, Alice, *For Your Own Good: Cruelty in Child-Rearing and the Roots of Violence*, New York, Farrar, Straus & Giroux, 2002.

Salomé, Jacques, *À qui ferais-je de la peine si j'étais moi-même? Comment renoncer à nos autosaboteurs*, Montréal, Éditions de l'Homme, 2008.

Schützenberger Ancelin, Ann, *Psycho-généalogie. Guérir les blessures familiales et se retrouver soi*, Paris, Petite bibliothèque Payot, 2015.

Schutzenberger, Ancelin, *The Ancestor Syndrome: Transgenerational Psychotherapy and the Hidden Links in the Family Tree*. USA, Routledge, 2014.

Urman, Valérie, *La Révolution épigénétique*, Paris, Albin Michel, 2018.

Acknowledgments

I wish to express my thanks…

Warm-heartedly, to all of my clients and friends whose experiences have inspired me and allowed me to grow with them, for "we are all teachers."

Affectionately, to my husband, Stéphan Pelletier, for the everlasting support that he has shown me throughout the process of writing this new edition as well as those that came before, and for bringing me peace of mind.

Unconditionally, to Jocelyne Lauzon, a psychologist with whom I worked for years on my self-esteem during the stormiest times of my life. To all of the teachers that I have followed on my journey of self-discovery.

Particularly, to the late Danielle Laporte, a psychologist whose sudden passing refueled more than ever my desire to be the best version of my true self.

Respectfully, to Germain Duclos, a friend to begin with, as well as a true humanist and specialist for whom I have a profound regard. Thank you for agreeing to read my work and for providing me with advice. To his editor, CHU Ste-Justine, for permitting me to use a chart which was essential to my message for parents.

Faithfully, to my reading committee for their precious feedback: to my eldest daughter, Geneviève Payette, my friends: Claudette, Hélène, Suzanne, Marguerite and Valerie. To my youngest, Julie Payette, who brightened up this book with her original "flower of self-esteem." For the new edition: Martin Denis, Hélène Duclos, Richard Fillion, Hassina Haid and Renée Ouimet.

Endlessly, to my French editor "Un monde différent", for making this very first dream, which was so close to my heart, come true. To Lise Labbé for her patience, and to Michel Ferron, for lighting the fire that sparked this new, updated and expanded edition. My deepest gratitude to Clara Daigneault who worked hard and smart to restore and transform a project draft in a professional English outcome: a dream of 20 years for me.

About enyla

Enyla, the pen name of Aline Lévesque, M.B.A., is a specialist in the development of human potential, having first studied in Industrial Relations at the
University of Montréal before completing her masters in Business Administration at the University of Québec at Montréal, where she specialized in
human relations and organizational behavior.

Co-founder and vice president of an association of counselors that help
clients in developing self-esteem, she also collaborates with a Québec mental
health organization. She was a Member of the International Self-Esteem
Council.

She has authored numerous self-help books focusing on self-esteem and
life purpose, and most recently, her first spiritual novel.

An excellent speaker as well as a writer, Aline has shared her talents by
leading talks and training sessions all over Québec, Canada, France, and
California.

Aline is known for her direct approach, sense of humor and vivacious
personality. She frequently makes use of items (scarves, puppets, etc.) to
conceptualize her ideas, which she expresses in a dynamic, straightforward
and meaningful way.

Aline's teachings mainly focus on **positive attitudes, potential, autonomy,
self-esteem and spirituality**. With her guidance, you will be sure to achieve
a deeper level of self-awareness.

For more information, you may contact her at:

www.alinelevesque.com
or
www.enyla.ca